VINTAGE
MISSOURI

VINTAGE MISSOURI

■ ■ ■ ■ ■

A GUIDE TO MISSOURI WINERIES

ROBERT F. SCHEEF

THE PATRICE PRESS

■ ■ ■ ■ ■

ST. LOUIS

To Leslie C. Engel
for bringing it all back home

© 1991
The Patrice Press

Library of Congress
Cataloging-in-Publication Data

Scheef, Robert F.
    Vintage Missouri: a guide to Missouri
wineries / Robert F. Scheef.
        p. 161   cm.
    ISBN 0-935284-90-7
    1. Wine and wine making—Missouri.
    I. Title.
    TP557.S28   1991
    663'.2'09778—dc20   91-25987
                                                     CIP

With thanks, the author acknowledges the hospitality of
Missouri winemakers and the interest of Jim Ashby,
Patrick Byers, Susan Carlson, Susie Riggin, and the
reference librarians of the St. Louis County Library and
the Missouri Historical Society.

Design: Mark Heitman

Cover photograph: Cynthiana grapes by Bill Fitch,
Montelle Winery

Printed in the United States of America

CONTENTS

Return
to
Missouri

ON RETURNING HOME TO ST. LOUIS IN 1989, MY
wife, Leslie, and I sadly said goodbye to the San
Francisco Bay area. We had enjoyed many unique
qualities of life in that special place. The consistency of
the climate, the beauty of postcard-perfect scenes surrounding us, the magnificence of the city's modern ar-
chitecture, the charm of its Victorian homes, and the
spunk of its inhabitants had captivated us and easily involved us in the swirl and clamor of the California
lifestyle.

Even with abundant amusements to distract us there,
we nonetheless admitted that we missed our home state.
We reminisced about the change of seasons that can hap-
pen in the passage of a single day, the smell of snowfall,
and the fearsome power of a thunderstorm hurtling
toward Illinois. We recalled float trips on chilled Ozark
streams during blistering summer months. Most of all,
we yearned for the love and kinship of family and old
friends. Thinking about our childhoods in Missouri, we
felt privileged: We had grown up in the heart of the country, insulated from the quirky fads that splash against
the nation's coastlines.

Among other activities that we left behind in California, we regretted giving up day trips to the wine country. Our standard tour for visitors had always included
a drive from cool, breezy San Francisco to the hot, dry
vineyards of Napa and Sonoma counties. We learned
to love California wine; more than that, we learned to
love wine in California and to appreciate it as a complement to our special dinners. Our fascination with

California wines led us to sample Italian, French, and German varieties. We became acquainted with the differences offered by the fruit of each region, the differences in each bottle we tasted.

We fully expected our wine-touring days to end when we came back to St. Louis. When we had moved away from home more than fifteen years ago, Missouri winemaking had a dubious reputation. More often than not, Missouri wine came from fruit that grew on bushes or trees and was bottled in tinted Ball jars. In terms of viscosity and taste, these country curios accompanied toast or peanut butter better than dinner.

This condition was not entirely the fault of grape growers in the state. Consumers bore an equal responsibility for determining what passed as wine in Missouri. My own parents, for example, kept their wine collection on a shelf under the silverware drawer in the kitchen. They stocked a Mogen David, a Bardenheier's Pale Dry Cocktail Sherry, and a musty green bottle of questionable origin and content. A few bottles of hard stuff rounded out this assortment to see them through any crisis in entertaining. For my folks, the Bardenheier's served as a year-round, all-occasion cocktail, *aperitif,* table wine, and nightcap. Their concoctions were simple: straight or on the rocks.

Soon after our return to Missouri, Leslie and I planned a fall foliage tour along the Missouri River. Fall—such as we had not experienced for a number of years— brought relief from the dog days of August that had first welcomed us. The startling colors in the trees alerted us to the fact that we now lived in a land where winters were freezing cold, spring renewed life, summers lasted forever, and the pennant stretch was nearly always hot.

Our route along Highway 100 took us to Hermann on the final weekend of the Oktoberfest. Over the eighty or so miles we drove that day, more than a half-dozen wineries beckoned from hand-painted signs at the side of the road. Still partly Californians, we were at first amused; but as native Missourians, we had to say, ''Show me!''

Though the wine routes of Napa and Sonoma offer

wineries as densely packed as shops in a mall, California wines had never lured us with names like Seyval Blanc, Chancellor, and Cynthiana. The Missouri names intrigued us; the tasting rooms welcomed us with conviviality unsurpassed by our West Coast hosts; and the wine impressed us as . . . well, to be honest, as different. Attractively labeled, proudly served, the wines were nonetheless different in a way that was hard to describe. Differences aside, we had to admit they tasted good.

In Missouri, grocery stores, liquor outlets, and restaurants carry a limited selection of California wines. Like cut flowers, they are often expensive. Most frequently, shelves display only Gallo, Almaden, and Paul Masson. Specialty shops tout a selection of Mondavi, Beaulieu Vineyard, Fetzer, Lytton Springs, and Stag's Leap. But where are the wines of small, family-owned vineyards? The ones that produce under 5,000 cases? The ones discovered on a wine tour? The lovely, surprising ones that never promise more than they can deliver? The hand-made wines? In the fifteen years since Leslie and I left Missouri, these wineries have cropped up in Missouri like jonquils through wet spring soil.

As Leslie and I continue our wine-tasting hobby in Missouri, we do so merely as tourists, claiming no pedigree of connoisseurship. More than recommending and prescribing what wines to drink—much less how to enjoy them—this book aims to reveal the renaissance of Missouri winemaking. On a personal level, we wish to share the joy of discovery that awaits those who venture into Missouri's wine country.

ROOTS
OF THE
VINE

"With the growth of the grape every nation elevates itself to a higher grade of civilization—brutality must vanish, and human nature progresses."

Friedrich Muench
School for American Grape Culture

MISSOURI HAS A LONG AND RESPECTED HISTORY as a winemaking state. Although Prohibition nearly erased that part of our past from memory, for half a century Missouri produced more wine than any other state outside of California. One hundred years ago its wineries brought home awards in international competition. Cynthiana, a native grape cultivated virtually nowhere else, produced a red wine that secured Missouri's reputation as a prominent winemaking region of distinguished and distinctive character.

In the current revival of winemaking in Missouri, enthusiastic writers give the impression that early settlers came to this region with the express purpose of making gold-medal wines. It has been suggested that on seeing the Missouri River valley, the pioneers thought first of planting vineyards. However, Missouri actually acquired the moniker of ''America's Rhineland'' only in the last half of the nineteenth century, when its output of wine surpassed Ohio's.

INTO THE WILDERNESS

Our history books tell us that the first Europeans arrived in the heartland of the continent with other ideas in mind than the cultivation of the fruit of the vine. Viniculture—that is, winegrowing—began as a garden agriculture closely associated with certain ethnic groups who brought to the region the skills and experience to vinify grapes, and, more importantly, a culture that respected wine as an important part of meals.

Arriving more than a century before the winemakers, however, Spanish adventurers came up the Mississippi River looking for gold and silver. They found lead instead and left. French missionaries, explorers, and trappers—the colorful *coureurs de bois* and *voyageurs*—followed soon after. While they did not discover a river route to the Orient, they nonetheless found abundant wildlife and dense hardwood forests strung with vines.

The land, especially the rolling hills south of the Missouri River, discouraged farming—not that these adventurers would have wanted to till the earth. Streams wrinkled the craggy hills with deep, verdant valleys. A plateau of scrub swelled southwest of the confluence of the Missouri and the Mississippi rivers and west of the rich floodplain at the mouth of the Ohio. Limestone, dolomite, and flint layered this dome like collapsed pottery. Wet winters and long summers spawned tangled thickets of the tenacious plants that could penetrate its surface, including wild grapes unfamiliar to Europeans.

The first permanent settlement in Missouri was at Ste. Genevieve circa 1749, soon followed by one in New Madrid to the south. Across the river from the earlier French outposts of Fort de Chartres and Kaskaskia, Ste. Genevieve attracted the commerce of farmers from Illinois who tilled the rich bottomland. Throughout the French and Spanish territorial period, any inclination of settlers to make wine from the grapes they found growing in the area earned the ire of government leaders who feared competition with the wine industry at home.

The next boost to the population west of the Mississippi came years later as a result of the French and Indian War. The terms of the ensuing Treaty of Paris of 1763 granted England most of the territory east of the Mississippi, including parts of Canada. To avoid the rule of Anglican Britain, many of the Illinois French crossed the river into Louisiana territory. The war also produced an agreement between France and Spain whereby Spain acquired Louisiana, the territory west of the river, as a gift and token of abiding friendship from France.

As a result of the American Revolution the United States took title to most of the British territory east of the Mississippi. The emerging nation presented an almost limitless frontier to Americans who hungered for the adventure, wide-open spaces, and natural resources no longer found in the Eastern Seaboard states. With a land grant from the government of Spanish Louisiana, Daniel Boone renounced his American citizenship to take up residence at the mouth of the Femme Osage Creek in 1797. Like-minded individuals pushed westward along Missouri and Meramec river routes, trapping and mining as they went.

TIME OF DISCOVERY

With the Louisiana Purchase in 1804 the administration of Thomas Jefferson divided the territory into Upper and Lower Louisiana, with the southern border of present-day Arkansas being the dividing line. Americans in the eastern states wanted to know every detail about the new land. With a charge from Jefferson, Meriwether Lewis and William Clark embarked on a mission to explore the farthest reaches of the Missouri River. Ten days out of St. Louis in 1804, Clark noted in his *Journal* the "last settlement of whites on this river" at the French village of La Charette, near present-day Marthasville.

After Lewis and Clark, the expeditions of Zebulon Montgomery Pike, then of Stephen H. Long in 1819, also sent back remarkable descriptions of the primeval areas west of the Mississippi. Chronicled by Dr. Edwin James in his 1823 *Account of an Expedition from Pittsburgh to the Rocky Mountains,* Long's party encountered a number of French and old-stock Americans along the Gasconade River en route to Council Bluffs on the Missouri River. Long might have coined the term "Ozark Mountains" to describe the topographical uplift south of the Missouri River, interpreting the French trappers' name for the region, *aux arcs*, meaning "in the country of the Arkansas," or "with bows," to describe the Quapaw branch of the Kansa tribe that occupied the region.

EARLIEST VINTAGES

Henry Marie Brackenridge, an early visitor to the Territory of Missouri, published in 1814 an account of his two-year stay in Ste. Genevieve called *Views of Louisiana.* Disclaiming a regional wine much touted by earlier visitors, Brackenridge wrote:

> Formerly a wretched sort of wine was made of the winter grape, but which is at present almost neglected. These vintages were never considered of much importance. The wine was made by bruising the grapes in a large tub; a heavy stone was then placed on them to press out the juice, which flowed through an opening at the bottom into a vessel prepared for its reception.

A footnote to the text mentions two kinds of grapes supposedly unique to the upper Mississippi valley at the time: *Vitis aestivalis* and *Vitis riparia*, strange new species to the European catalog of known plants. Distinctive native grapes of the Missouri River valley included Brackenridge's "winter grape," possibly *Vitis cordifolia,* and an unnamed white grape.

In the period before Missouri's statehood, French missionaries had established outposts in the wilderness from which to spread the Gospel. Existing documents date the Church of St. Ferdinand to 1792. In 1818 Bishop William Du Bourg bought a 205-acre farm that abutted the Missouri River. By his gift, the Jesuits founded St. Stanislaus Novitiate on the "Bishop's Farm" near the bluffs of the Missouri River. One of the state's earliest recorded vintages was crushed around 1823 at the self-sufficient Jesuit seminary to provide wine for celebrating the Eucharist. Although wild grapes grew abundantly in the "flowering valley" near the Missouri River, the St. Stanislaus brothers and students mostly made *vinum e malis*, "wine from apples," or cider, until the late 1800s.

SEEDS OF COMMUNITY

A community of twenty Swiss-German families settled the Whitewater River area near Cape Girardeau in 1780. In contrast to "old-stock" Americans like Boone, these immigrants likely brought winemaking skills with them from the old country. By 1817 the Whitewater River area consisted of "an isolated but pure German settlement," according to Rev. Timothy Flint who ascended the Mississippi on his way to St. Charles. Among other observations, Flint noted in his *Reflections* several examples of excessive drinking by prominent members—even the German pastor—of this community.

The flow of settlers into Missouri, starting as a tentative trickle in the eighteenth century, became a river of optimistic farmers following statehood in 1821. European immigrants, principally Germans, swelled the throng by millions in the second quarter of the nineteenth century. They tarried in the coastal cities that received them only long enough to establish the compass bearing that would lead them to the storied heartland and pastures of plenty.

Trappers and explorers had already named the rivers and landforms, building havens of safety and supply along the westward route. The new tide of immigrants faithfully followed these road signs. Yet, unlike the free-spirited individualists who had carved the trails in search of the measure of this seemingly limitless land, the settlers sought fertile soil in which to plant the seeds of community. They dreamed of an abundance of rich cropland available from the government at homesteader prices. This dream itself was sufficient reason for them to forsake their native land; they also dreamed of liberty.

In the years following the Napoleonic Wars, Germany consisted of a confederation of independent and sometimes fractious states. The reigning monarchs of Austria, Prussia, and the smaller German duchies resolved to thwart the trend toward constitutional democracy inspired by revolutions in America and France. In addition to censorship and repressive new laws, severe taxation and limited—if any—representation in government led to widespread discontent and a series of uprisings. Many Germans also resented mandatory military service for men. In practice, anyone who had enough money could avoid this obligation by hiring a surrogate to serve instead. In the countryside and rural villages, protesters sang the praises of America, the land of the free where all were equal from birth.

Added to the chafing of strict authoritarian control, the early stages of industrialization attacked the income from cottage industries on which so many peasant families had come to depend. Regarding themselves as farmers, now with a bleak future in the industrialized cities, the landless tenant farmers considered two options: Move east in a desperate search for farmland or immigrate to America. For tens of thousands, often whole communities, immigration to America appeared as a gamble worth taking. They hoped to regain their agrarian heritage and the independence of farming.

A VISITOR FROM GERMANY

In 1824 Gottfried Duden, civil servant and one-time medical student, set out from Remscheid in the Rhine Valley Duchy of Berg to see the New World for himself. Accompanied by Louis Eversmann, Duden followed the Ohio River to the new state of Missouri. Believing that overpopulation had become the root of many political and social ills in Europe, Duden and Eversmann sought inexpensive government land that immigrating Germans could clear and farm. They ended their sojourn west of St. Louis near Femme Osage Creek and the Missouri River, becoming neighbors of the family of the fabled Daniel Boone.

In addition to bargain rates for land there, Duden also found an appealing systems of waterways. He knew that settlers coming into the wilderness, especially farmers, would rely on the river for access to markets and for news from the rest of the world. In this way, the Missouri River was potentially as great an asset to the region as the Rhine in Duden's homeland.

Over a period of more than two years, Duden farmed in the Femme Osage region. Hired help allowed him to concentrate his attention on the many natural attributes of his adopted home. He recorded his observations about America in a series of letters that he published in Germany in 1829. Many German readers considered as hardly more credible than fantasy his travelog and treatise, *Report on a Journey to the Western States of North American and a Stay of Several Years Along the Missouri.*

While travel literature had become a popular form of escape for Germans, Duden's *Report* stood out as the "everything-you-ever-wanted-to-know-about" guide to emigration. Duden articulated the hopes of his German readers when he unabashedly proclaimed: "For there is no opportunity in overpopulated Germany. In North America, however, every possible one exists."

Duden barely restrained his enthusiasm for the paradise that he found on the Missouri River. As if to reassure the tenant farmers of his native land, Duden explained the importance of agriculture in the new democracy: "But everywhere farming is a respected occupation and the highest official of the state would not hesitate to do manual labor on his own farm.''

About winegrowing specifically Duden told the Rhinelanders back home that ''grape vines whose trunks, over a foot thick, rise up about a hundred feet, free as cables, and then spread out in the crowns of elms with their heavily foliaged vines.'' He offhandedly added that ''some hills are so densely covered by them that wagonloads of grapes can be gathered in a short time.''

In contrast to the opportunities offered by such abundance, however, Duden hinted that Americans did not share the tradition of wine that every German respected as part of the evening meal. Duden cautioned those who thought of growing grapes:

> Grapevines, rape oil, and poppy seed oil have, no matter how much their culture may promise, not found the slightest attention either in the state of Missouri or in bordering countries. As to wine, grapes have always been imported from warmer regions. Also, the descendants of the British do not understand viniculture, and those descended from other people have not learned it from their parents.

Despite the difficulties that Duden pointed out about winegrowing in the United States, he nonetheless remained optimistic about the possibilities of this form of agriculture. ''For immigrants from the Rhineland nothing is more important than viniculture,'' he wrote. ''They do not need to worry about a ready market and high prices. For the Americans look upon viniculture as a national matter, saying the Old World has nothing to offer them except wine.''

As an illustration of the role of wine in contemporary American culture, Duden related his experience in the Dufour settlement of Vevay, Indiana, where he stopped on his way to Missouri. He noted that the community began from a land grant issued by Congress around the turn of the century. To the Swiss families who had accepted the terms of the grant, Congress had stipulated that they engage in viticulture. Duden assessed the wine he tasted there as ''poor enough.''

On an expedition of another sort, Jean Jacques

Dufour came to America from Vevey, Switzerland, in 1796, lured by the commercial potential of supplying fine wine to the sophisticated gentry of this young nation. Often had he read the lament of Revolutionary War generals and prominent politicians who had no wine to accompany their meals. He investigated several promising vineyard locations between St. Louis and Kaskaskia, finding scant evidence of the Jesuit vineyards in the latter place.

Following a quick survey of Cape Girardeau, Dufour chose first to settle on the Kentucky side of the Ohio River. More than ten difficult years passed before he finally abandoned *Fiersnewyard,* his "First Vineyard," which had been ravaged by frost and pests. He and his family then moved into Indiana and planted the hearty Alexander grape, known as the Cape grape, an accidental cross between a wild, indigenous species and a cultivated, winemaking variety imported from Europe. In Vevay, Indiana, Dufour became a leading authority on viticulture in the United States for his *American Vine Dresser's Guide* and conducted experiments in his vineyards until his death in 1826.

While Gottfried Duden extolled the virtues of agriculture, he acknowledged that other concerns weighed on the minds of his German readers. Overpopulation in Europe had first driven him to satisfy his wanderlust. Educated members of German society had other reasons for emigrating. The ideal of liberty embroidered an appealing theme throughout Gottfried Duden's Report as well as in other accounts of the United States by early nineteenth century writers. This yearning for freedom inspired liberal-thinking readers to form emigration collectives. By pooling their resources, the members of these groups organized and funded the immigration of a colony that shared the same principles.

LATIN FARMERS

In 1832 Baron Wilhelm Johann von Bock led a group of freedom-loving intellectuals of the Berlin Society straight to Duden country, founding the town of Dutzow, Missouri. A visitor to the von Bock farm in 1833 described the baron as "the soul of the colony," which he named after his former estate in Mecklenberg-Schwerin. Many of the aristocrats who joined von Bock in America did not have the background to succeed as pioneer farmers. Dismayed by difficulties, not a few members of the group returned to Germany.

Led by Friedrich Muench and Paul Follenius, the Giessen Society typified the organized emigration efforts. Classmates at the University of Giessen, Muench and Follenius had gained notoriety as radicals. The failure of the 1830 revolution convinced them to form an emigration collective. With high ideals and optimism, the members of the Giessen Society bought passage to America in 1834. On its arrival, however, the group dissolved its formal organization.

As individuals Muench and Follenius pressed on to Duden's paradise. Muench, a Lutheran minister, became a prominent political voice in his new surroundings, winning a seat in the Missouri state senate in 1862. He also planted vineyards near Dutzow in Warren County and earned the reputation as a viticultural expert for his *School for American Grape Culture*. He died in December 1881 at the age of eighty-three while tending his vineyard.

These leaders of German colonies came to be known as ''Latin farmers'' in deference to their education and social standing. In addition to their love of liberty, the Latin farmers romanticized agrarian life and values, though before immigrating they hardly knew anything about farming.

A NEW GERMAN STATE

In 1836 the *Deutsche Ansiedlungs Gesellshaft zu Philadelphia* proclaimed this as their goal: to establish a new fatherland in America. The German Settlement Society began searching for a place where they could insulate their community from the influences of the American melting pot. Hearing of the vast expance of available land across the Mississippi, they turned their attention from Philadelphia to the western frontier. The wish of some members of the organization to form a new German state was not impossible.

The German language newspapers of eastern and European cities discussed the society's plans in great detail. This news attracted dues-paying supporters from many states east of the Mississippi as well as Canada. By April 1837 the society had collected enough funds from stockholders to launch an expedition. In addition to immediate access to a navigable river, the perfect location was to have conditions ''advantageous to the growing of grain, wine and fruit and to the raising of cattle and sheep.'' They envisioned a place where the manufacturing enterprises of a town would work in tandem with outlying farms to create a diversified economic base for the shareholders.

In three months the search party returned to Philadelphia, positive that they had found the ideal location for the colony. It was more than a coincidence that the representatives of the society had chosen, like Gottfried Duden, to follow the Missouri River westward from St. Louis. Traveling upstream toward the mouth of the Gasconade River, the scouting party noted a topography that favored diversified agriculture and waterborne commerce. As important as these features, the reasonable price for adequate acreage satisfied the criteria of the society's mission.

Winning the full approval of the society's executives, the agents returned to the mouth of the Gasconade and purchased slightly more than 11,000 acres on the south bank of the Missouri River. They platted lots for the new town adjacent to the river. As an emblem of its distinctive German character, the proposed city was named Hermann, a Romantic reference to the first century hero (known historically as Arminius) who led Germans to victory over Roman armies.

Deprivation, disease, and other hardships dogged the efforts of the first members of the German Settlement Society who arrived in Hermann in December 1837. In addition, arguments within the group and personal differences in this transitional period caused several settlers to write angry letters to the society's executives in Philadelphia. Nonetheless, a town began to take shape.

While remaining true to their goal of establishing a homogeneous German community, the first citizens of Hermann had to modify other expectations to suit the existing conditions. Their dream of basing the enterprise on the interlocking foundations of manufacturing and agriculture fell short on two accounts. First, scarce mineral deposits discouraged manufacturing ventures; and second, general agriculture was hampered by low-quality soil and the great distance that separated farms from the town.

HERMANN—FRUIT OF THE VINE

The first waves of settlers, French and old-stock Americans, had already claimed rich bottom lands and prairies, terrain more easily cultivated than the hills. The ridges and bluffs that abutted the river were cheaper than valley and prairie fields and lifted the inhabitants from the malaria plagues that often vanquished those on the lowland farms. Because of these topographical features and the limitations of the soil, the trustees of the city of Hermann promoted viticulture. In exchange for easy payment plans and interest-free loans, buyers of city-owned tracts agreed to plant vineyards on the ''wine lots.''

Winegrowing in Hermann succeeded for other reasons as well. German farming techniques stressed the efficient use of even marginally arable land. Where other crops would have been difficult to tend, rows of vines grew easily on the slopes of hills that rose up from the Missouri River. When the people of Hermann looked around, they were well pleased by such efficient use of the land and warmly reminded of the winegrowing regions of their homeland.

In addition, their Old World customs readily accepted winegrowing as a respected agriculture. They associated none of the taboos with alcohol that many old-stock Americans carried with them. To the German immigrants, wine and beer occupied a place on the family dinner table alongside platters of sauerbraten and spaetzle. In contrast, their English-speaking neighbors, transplants from Appalachia and the South, regarded drinking as an exclusively male activity with one main purpose: to become drunk. To these folk it was far easier to manufacture distilled spirits from abundant grains than to cultivate the vine and vinify its fruit. German immigrants built their *Weingärten* as places for families to dine and socialize, whereas immigrants from the British Isles built their pubs as retreats from family life.

Moreover, the German immigrants experimented methodically and doggedly with a variety of cultivars that had found disfavor or disaster in the vineyards of Ohio and New York. In tribute to their success in cultivating this culturally significant agricultural product, the people of Hermann celebrated by holding their first grape harvest festival in 1848. In that year, Hermann wineries produced 10,000 gallons of wine.

WINE FROM THE LAND

Gert Goebel, the son of a Giessen Society member, visited Hermann's first *Weinfest* and included his evaluation of the wine he sampled in *Länger als ein Menschenleben in Missouri (Longer than a Lifetime in Missouri)*. He described a wine made by Michael Poeschel as ''a very expensive but good Catawba, which, when it is treated right, resembles Rhinewine very closely.'' A native of Altenburg in the German state of Saxony, Poeschel had erected the Poeschel Winery in 1847, becoming an immediate leader in the town's burgeoning wine industry. He later brought John Scherer into the business and renamed the firm Poeschel & Scherer. In 1883 the winery became Stone Hill Wine Company under the leadership of William Herzog and George Stark. More than one hundred years after its founding, Poeschel's winery would reappear in the forefront of a reborn wine industry in Missouri.

Confident of the region's potential for winegrowing, the grape growers of Hermann banded together to form the Gascondade Grape Growing Society, the nation's first agricultural organization devoted entirely to the cultivation of the vine. By 1856 Hermann's production of wine had grown to 100,000 gallons. Beginning with Jacob Fugger's cultivation of Isabella and the Catawbas grown by his neighbors, vineyards adopted new varieties. Norton's Virginia Seedling became a strong favorite under the cultivation of vintner Jacob Rommel.

Born in Schaarndorf, Wuerttemberg, Rommel had received training as a winegrower in Germany. Later in his career he earned renown for hybrids developed in his nursery and his wines graced tables in St. Louis and New York.

George Husmann's parents brought him to Hermann as a ten-year-old in 1838. The family had fled their home in Meyenburg, Prussia, one of the most inflexible and autocratic states of the German Confederation. From planting his first vineyard in 1847, this man's significant contributions to winemaking included cultivating the Concord grape in Hermann and developing disease-resistant rootstock at his nursery. He authored several definitive books on viticulture and winemaking, edited the *Grape Culturist*, the nation's first periodical devoted only to viticulture, and regularly contributed essays on winegrowing to the reports of the United States Commissioner of Agriculture. He also held the first professorship of pomology (fruit growing) and forestry at the University of Missouri in 1878-1881, before taking his skills to Talcoa Vineyards in California's Napa Valley.

Franz Langendoerfer also played a prominent role in Hermann's winegrowing industry. He and his family arrived in 1848 from the winegrowing Rhine valley in the Grand Duchy of Baden. On his farm south of town Franz took advantage of a cave for storing his wine. Constructing a wall at the mouth of the cave, he named his winery "Langendoerfer Natural Cave Wine Cellar." Although August Loehnig, like Michael Poeschel, came from the east-central German state of Saxony, an area not known for its wines, he had been a vinedresser's son there. In 1859 Loehnig took up residence in a rock house east of Hermann while he worked for George Husmann. He later joined Husmann as partner, eventually buying Husmann's farm.

By trying different grapes, these vintners succeeded where their counterparts in Ohio and other eastern states had failed. Their success distinguished Hermann as a wine center and their nurseries supplied vines to growers throughout the country. In *Der Staat Missouri*, published in 1858, Friedrich Muench characterized the landscape south of the city as "amphitheatrically surrounded by chains of hills, from which the primeval forest has been cleared first in the last years in order to make room for vineyards which are increasing every year.''

Despite the tremendous success of winegrowing in Hermann, other newcomers to the Missouri River valley frequently adopted the farming practices and occupations of their American neighbors. Even though they clung to their native religious practices and many ethnic social customs, the immigrant farmers cleared their land for crops of more immediate need and commercial value than grapes. At first they planted the crops they needed for their survival, such as wheat and corn. With the success of these efforts, they then tried raising tobacco and cotton, crops that offered a profitable market value.

Through years of hardship and isolation, the early immigrants wrote letters to ease nearly overwhelming homesickness. Their reports greatly interested family members who had remained in Germany. A cause-and-effect relationship seemed to exist between the arrival of news from America and the decision to immigrate. Thus, virtually whole communities would pack up and leave over the period of 1820 to 1870. In this fifty-year span, nearly two-and-a-half million Germans landed in America. This ''chain migration'' had the effect of concentrating German families in Missouri communities such as Westphalia, Kaeltztown, Freeburg, and Dutchtown.

CULTURE OF THE FAITHFUL

One of the most important unifying elements of the transplanted communities was the church. The freedom to practice their religion provided a strong impetus for entire congregations to leave Germany. For example, many Roman Catholics left Muenster to settle around the Maries Creek area of Westphalia. Others joined the French settlement of Ste. Genevieve because of shared religious allegiance, eventually giving the community a strong German character. From Saxony in 1839, meanwhile, a communal Lutheran sect, the Stephanists, took up residence in Perry County, Missouri. The written aims of the sect mentioned vine culture as a means of sustaining their members. Along the Mississippi north of Cape Girardeau they built towns such as Wittenburg, Frohna, Paitzdorf (later renamed Uniontown), and

Altenburg. This last site became the cradle of Missouri Synod Lutheranism in Trinity Lutheran Church and the original location of Concordia Seminary, now in St. Louis.

Protestant Waldensians, known as Savoyards, emigrated from the region of France bordering Italy because of religious persecution. After an unsuccessful investigation of conditions in Uruguay, the group answered advertisements placed by the St. Louis-San Francisco railroad that offered land near Monett in Barry County in the southwest part of the state. Following the initial settlement of the Savoyard community in 1875, other Waldensian families arrived in this example of chain migration. Like the Rhinelanders who settled near Westphalia, the Savoyards brought a winegrowing tradition with them to Missouri, cultivating grapes for the family table.

TRAILS OF SILVER RAILS

A factor that made chain migration feasible and contributed to the growth of a European population in Missouri was the rise of steam-powered transportation. Prior to 1840, trans-Atlantic passage took two months by sail. Steam power shortened the trip to two weeks. In addition, railroads sped the new arrivals into the hinterland of the country, populating freshly laid rail routes.

From St. Louis, immigrant expansion in the second half of the nineteenth century followed trails of silver rails. Railroad settlements like that of the Savoyards grew up around the Springfield area soon after the end of the Civil War. Railroad companies promoted the temperate climate and inexpensive land along their routes. This promise lured Swiss, French, Swedish, and Austrian nationals as well as immigrants who had first experienced the severity of the American winter in Great Lakes states.

In the history of the southwest and central regions of Missouri, the railroad settlements played a key role in the state's winemaking heritage. Even before the Civil War, as possible transcontinental routes were being discussed and entertained in several cities in the nation's heartland, railroad officials saw clearly the benefits of overland steam transportation to the embryonic grape industry in Missouri. Missouri's state geologist, George Clinton Swallow, surveyed proposed rail routes in the 1850s. In addition to noting topography and natural resources, Swallow also emphasized the suitability of the land for viticulture, then a highly promising form of agriculture. On an expedition from St. Louis to Neosho along the planned southwestern branch of the Pacific Railroad, Swallow recorded an abundance of wild grape species throughout the state.

In 1858 the chief engineer of the Pacific of Missouri, Edward Miller, painted a glowing picture of the future of Boonville as a center of winegrowing. By cultivating the vine, he said, ''the demon of intemperance is exorcised from Missouri by substituting the mild and wholesome juice of the grape for the fiery and poisonous product of the still.'' By 1859 the vintners of the ''Vine Clad City,'' as Boonville was then known, were producing upward of 6,000 gallons of wine annually, mostly from the Boonville Wine Company.

After the Civil War, a number of rail enterprises resumed their plans to cross the Great Plains. No less a public figure than John C. Fremont, lionized as ''the Pathfinder'' for his adventures with Kit Carson, incorporated the Atlantic & Pacific Railroad Company in 1866. At that time, the war-ravaged rail route had progressed only as far as Rolla, a far cry from the goldfields of California and the riches of the Orient. Unable to attract many buyers of land alongside the Atlantic & Pacific right-of-way, Fremont enlisted the assistance of the American Emigrant Aid & Homestead Company in promoting the tracts to immigrating Europeans. Using its own steamship line, the American Emigrant Company brought boatloads of Swedes and Danes to America where they were quickly shunted onto trains bound for Missouri.

The Atlantic & Pacific and the other railroads that later evolved into the ''Frisco Line'' held one business practice in common: They would sell land adjacent to the rail line to offset construction costs and bolster the initially small net returns from freight and passenger traffic. To this end, the Frisco posted handbills that touted the convenience and fertility of farmland along their routes. Such advertisements attracted a group of French families to Phelps County. Hailing from a place near the border with Switzerland, these immigrants began cultivating grapes in Dillon, a point midway between Rolla and St. James, in the 1870s.

Certainly they found wine grapes in cultivation by German settlers in Phelps County. Conrad E. Soest reported that he and his neighbors, Neumann and Stahr, had planted about twenty-five acres in Catawba, Concord, and Norton in 1870.

VINO DI ITALIA

In the closing years of the nineteenth century, the Frisco made a similar contribution to the growth of a winemaking industry in Missouri. A group of Italians had been lured to this country to grow cotton as sharecroppers in eastern Arkansas. Facing immediate adversity, including a severe outbreak of malaria, the group scattered soon after its arrival. Since few of the disillusioned survivors had enough money to return to Italy, representatives of the group set off in search of more tolerable circumstances. Father Pietro Bandini led the largest faction to Tontitown in northwestern Arkansas, where vineyards soon appeared.

Earlier, a smaller group of families, originally from the northern Italian region of Vicenza, looked to Missouri. Following a brief stopover with southern Italians in St. Louis, the weary travelers purchased land from the Frisco in 1898 at a place near St. James in Phelps County. To populate this newly laid rail route the railroad company offered the Italians land for as little as a dollar per acre.

Arriving virtually destitute, the newcomers set themselves to clearing the land. Determined to entwine their future with this land, the Italians planted fruit trees and other crops that did not yield immediately. To make ends meet, some cut timber for sale as railroad ties or performed other temporary labor for the Frisco.

Like the Germans, the Italians also regarded wine as food for the table. In one version of the story, the Frisco's

French colony at Dillon welcomed the newest arrivals to Missouri with cuttings of the Concord grapes. In any case, the Italians planted their vineyards in 1905 and named their new home Knobview to describe the uplifts of land on the prairie around their community. Some twenty years later, they took the name of Rosati for their town to honor Joseph Rosati, bishop of the diocese of St. Louis from 1827 to 1843.

Even though the soil and climate of the Ozark highlands seemed to be less than perfect for viticulture—at least as the Italians knew viticulture—they found some success in cultivating the native Concord variety. They started by planting a few cultivars in the household garden, a feature reminiscent of the homes they had left in their native land. Like so many nineteenth century immigrants from continental Europe, these Italians brought with them winemaking skills and a respect for wine as an integral part of the dinner setting.

As the population of the state and its reputation as a winegrowing area grew, other immigrants arrived with plans to set out vineyards in the "Missouri Rhineland." On the solid ground of a viable, though young, vineyard agriculture, winemakers brought Missouri to its peak years as a winegrowing state in the late 1800s.

VINE-
YARDS
IN
BLOOM

VITICULTURE IN MISSOURI FLOWERED AND BORE fruit in the second half of the nineteenth century. In extraordinary numbers the immigrants who carried a winemaking tradition as part of their cultural baggage found fertile ground in the state. While the rich soil along the river did not necessarily discourage the cultivation of staple crops, vineyards thrived on marginally arable slopes just as Gottfried Duden had predicted. The bluffs and gently rolling hills resembled the Rhine Valley and basked in sunshine through long summer months. Harsh winters and mysterious pest infestations, however, made the cultivation of Old World wine varieties— Chardonnay, Pinot Noir, Cabernet Sauvignon, Riesling, and the like—all but impossible.

Nonetheless, farmers planted grapes, at first in the family garden with other foods of the table. Where varieties from Europe quickly failed, the fruit of native *Vitis labrusca*—meaning "wild vine"—crowded the tendrils of gangly vines. As early as the mid-seventeenth century, the colonists had called it "the fox grape," probably to capture in words a musky, wild aroma; thus, they described the strongly flavored *labrusca* wine as "foxy," a term equivalent to the word "gamey" used to characterize wild meat. At best, the flavor of the grape overpowered the lingering pungency of the fox-grape wine. At worst, the smell encouraged comparison to wet fur.

Alexander Kayser, a St. Louis lawyer, suggested the potential of Missouri wines as early as 1849. In *The Western Journal* of that year, Kayser offered monetary prizes for the best wines of 1849, 1850, and 1851. The first year's winner would bear the honorary appellation "The Ore Blossom" in recognition of Missouri's mineral resources. The vintage 1850 and 1851 winners would be labeled "The Viaticum" and "The Free Soil Florescence," respectively. Not unexpectedly, Jacob Rommel of Hermann took the first year's purse with his Catawba entry.

Missouri's wine output grew from a modest ten thousand gallons in 1849 to nearly two million gallons in 1879.

After surpassing Ohio's production in the 1860s, Missouri held a solid second place to California until Prohibition. (With completion of the first transcontinental railroad in 1869, California was able to supply eastern markets with the familiar and much-sought-after European-type wines and to compete with wines made in Missouri, Ohio, New York, and elsewhere.)

NEW WORLD OF GRAPES

East of the Rocky Mountains, agronomists closely studied the ways of the native vine, confident of their region's winegrowing potential. Horticulturists crossed native species with Europe's and grafted the two together, hoping to breed plants that could withstand Missouri's unpredictable winters while at the same time yield a fine wine with "noble" European characteristics.

Through arduous experimentation that sometimes obscured a plant's genealogy, researchers identified a few native varieties that showed particular promise on their own. Norton's Virginia Seedling, for example, came to Missouri around 1838. Friedrich Muench credited a man named Widersprecher, one of the early Hermann settlers, with bringing the first cuttings from Virginia by way of Cincinnati. Jacob Rommel, the Hermann winegrower who first vinified Norton grapes, said he received his cuttings from George Riefensthal, a member of the first contingent of Philadelphia Germans to settle in Hermann. Growers referred to the hardy black grape as Norton's Virginia Seedling in recognition of Dr. Daniel Norton who had cultivated this member of *Vitis aestivalis* in Richmond, Virginia.

Closely resembling the Virginia Seedling, Cynthiana, or the "Red River grape," arrived from Ohio some time later, according to Muench's *School for American Grape Culture*. Other prominent viticulturists, such as George Husmann, placed its origins in Arkansas. This grape's mysterious history and its similarity to Norton's Virginia Seedling sparked an ongoing debate about whether these members of *V. aestivalis* were actually the same plant variety. Muench, Husmann, and other winemakers of the mid-1800s regarded the differences as discernible in terms of the sweetness and color of the wine each produced, as well as subtle physical characteristics. More important than the argument over classification, these *aestivalis* grapes thrived in Missouri and produced a wine of much less foxiness than *labrusca* grapes. Missouri winegrowers succeeded in earning a reputation for their skill based largely on this sturdy American species and won a gold medal for Cynthiana at the Vienna Exposition of 1873.

A prominent Texas horticulturist of the nineteenth century, Thomas Volney Munson (1843-1913) saw in that dry flatland promising conditions for successful viticulture. Munson collected indigenous grape species from virtually every state. Throughout a lifetime of experimentation, he developed over three hundred hybrid varieties. He named one of his hybrids for Friedrich Muench. This grape, probably a cross between South Carolina's Herbemont and the post oak grape, showed promise in the making of a crisp, dry red wine.

MISSOURI ROOTS IN EUROPE

Fate did not allow the American grape breeders to remain anonymous. In the second half of the nineteenth century, an insatiable pest was ravaging the vineyards of France. Acre by acre the tiny *Phylloxera vitifolia*—also known as *vastatrix,* the "devastator"—began attacking plant after plant, feeding on tender roots. Incapable of arresting its advance, French winegrowers wept over rows of plants that had severed their infested roots and died.

The infestation came at a time when French winemakers had reaped unprecedented profits from their vines. In the years after the Napoleonic Wars, new markets had spurred demand for French wine. Shortly thereafter, the advent of steam-powered transportation provided the means to supply these international markets. As a result, French farmers intensified vineyard plantings. They, like their American counterparts, also experimented with hybrid varieties, crossing their *V. vinifera* with strange, new species imported from the United States.

No one realized that the cuttings from the New World carried organisms unknown to Europe. Prior to steam travel, vines had arrived free of active insects. Ironically, while steam travel boosted access to new markets for the French, the shortened trans-Atlantic trip to Europe permitted the *Phylloxera* louse to survive. *Vitis vinifera* was as susceptible to *Phylloxera* as dry kindling to a spark.

Growers in France tried in vain to save their vines. They fumigated, injected chemicals into the soil, and even flooded their vineyards to drown the pest. Their toil achieved a barely noticeable slowing of the devastation. Near the end, salvation, like the louse itself, came from America.

At the time, Charles V. Riley, state entomologist for Missouri, was regarded as perhaps the world's foremost expert on many agricultural pests. Through his collaboration with Jules-Emile Planchon of France, the life cycle of this minute devastator was understood for the first time.

Riley determined that *Phylloxera* had survived in America without killing off its host by attaching to the tough stems and leaves where galls quickly formed. He suggested that grafting European cuttings onto American rootstock might enable the French vines to withstand the deadly attack. Questions about how the union would affect the quality of the grapes yielded to the desperation of the situation. With a noble national tradition at stake, the French were willing to try anything.

Heeding the call for help, Hermann Jaeger shipped seventeen carloads of native rootstock to Europe in the 1870s. Jaeger had immigrated to Missouri from Switzerland after the Civil War. In his vineyard near Neosho he developed hybrids of the Virginia Seedling. Working with George Husmann and Munson, Jaeger was optimistic that native American rootstock, principally cuttings of *Vitis rupestris* and *Vitis riparia*, would shield the classic vines of Europe from the fatal effects of the *Phylloxera* louse.

With these rootstocks sent by Jaeger, Husmann, and others, French growers were able to turn back the advance of *Phylloxera*. In recognition of their viticultural contributions, the French government awarded these two American scientists its Cross of the Legion of Honor in 1888. As an everlasting symbol of their appreciation, the city of Montpellier erected a statue that depicts the New

World as a young woman propping up an infirm old woman, France.

With barely a nod to Missouri, California winegrowers imported from France the disease-resistant rootstock that Jaeger, Munson, and others had shipped to Europe. In 1875 California produced four million gallons of wine. With *Phylloxera* under control, this output rose to fifteen million gallons in 1895.

TOP OF THE WORLD'S WINE LIST

Through to end of the nineteenth century and the early part of the twentieth, Missouri winemakers continued to win international awards for their wines while at the same time increasing production. According to the annual report of the Bureau of Labor in Missouri, the state produced more than three million gallons of wine in 1904, about eight percent of all wine produced for sale in the United States. Gasconade County by itself, mainly the city of Hermann, accounted for nearly all of this output.

Stone Hill Winery in particular won a place for Missouri on the world winemaking map, taking eight gold medals in international competitions in the last quarter of the nineteenth century. During its heyday as the second largest producer in the country, the winery vinified more than a million gallons of wine per year. In 1901 a bottle of Stone Hill champagne christened the first battleship *Missouri*.

Other wineries also contributed to Missouri's claim as a prominent winemaking region of the United States before Prohibition. George Husmann managed the Bluffton Wine Company across the Missouri River from Hermann in 1869. That same year President U. S. Grant ordered forty cases of the company's wines, including Cynthiana. In 1870 Bluffton's vineyard of more than 1,500 acres yielded 13,000 gallons of wine. The firm set up a business and distribution facility at 22-24 South Main Street in St. Louis.

In the late 1800s St. Louis formed the hub of wine manufacture and distribution in America. The Missouri Wine Company, founded in 1832, brought world-wide fame to the city and to Missouri wines. Acquired in 1859 by Chicago entrepreneur and politician Isaac Cook, the firm's Cook's Imperial Champagne became well-known throughout America and Europe. Using grapes from the northwest corner of Ohio, the winery, renamed the American Wine Company by Cook, produced 10,000 bottles a day in 1901. It cellared its inventory in huge vaults forty to fifty feet beneath its facility at the corner of Cass and Garrison streets. After the repeal of Prohibition in 1933, the winery again fell on hard times with the disclosure of its financial relationship with Joachim von Ribbentrop, Hitler's foreign minister. Following the demise of the firm in St. Louis, the owners moved to California and continued to make the famous Cook's Imperial Brut Champagne at the Korbel Winery.

Established in 1866 by Dr. C. W. Spalding, the Cliff Cave Wine Company converted a natural cave near the Mississippi River into a two-story wine cellar. Located near present-day Telegraph and Baumgartner roads in south St. Louis County, the winery produced 3,000 gallons of wine from twenty-five acres in 1870. In October of that year, it won the Best Norton diploma at the St. Louis Fair.

Isidor Bush & Co., also known as the American Wine Depot, vinified native grapes in St. Louis as early as 1869. In 1850, two years after emigrating from Prague, Isidor Bush had started business as a grocer. Turning attention to native grapes, the firm became widely known for its wines, winning a gold medal for its Cynthiana at the Vienna Exposition in 1873. A fire in 1882 forced the winery to relocate from 206 Fourth Street to 213-215 South Second Street.

In partnership with the Bush family, Gustave Edward Meissner sent native rootstock to France in 1877 from his vineyard on Meissner's Island in the Mississippi River. Born in 1843 in Muehlhausen, Germany, Meissner had arrived in St. Louis in 1868. In the course of his lifetime, Meissner became an acknowledged viticultural expert. His vineyard, across from Bushberg's Landing, a few miles upstream from Herculaneum in Jefferson County, grew a hundred varieties of grapes on six hundred acres.

Called *A Grape Growers' Manual,* the Bushberg catalog

published by Bush & Son & Meissner included essays by George Engelmann, one of the most prominent physicians of St. Louis and an avid botanist. Engelmann had immigrated to the United States in 1832, following the completion of his studies at the University of Wuerzburg. His classification of native vines raised the Bushberg nurseries' catalog to the level of required reading in many agricultural schools in this country. Translated into French and Italian, it functioned as a bible to even seasoned *vignerons* in Europe.

The Stone Hill Wine Company of Hermann also maintained business offices in St. Louis in the closing years of the nineteenth century. The winery annually distributed some 150,000 gallons through the Gateway City to wine lovers throughout the world. In a similar vein, the Napa and Sonoma Wine Company, located at 206-212 Olive Street, employed the port facilities of St. Louis to market wines from California. Established in 1863, this firm was the largest representative of California wines east of the Rockies.

Added to this list of prominent nineteenth century wineries in St. Louis, Bardenheier's Wine Cellars was one of the few winemaking firms nationwide to survive Prohibition. Established in 1873 as the John Bardenheier Wine and Liquor Company, huge cellars stretched beneath its location at 212-214 Market across from the St. Louis Cathedral (the "Old Cathedral"). The firm imported wine from Europe and vinified grapes from California, Ohio, and Missouri.

FRIEND HUSMANN

To further earn renown as the center of American viniculture in the late 1800s, St. Louis also introduced in 1869 the first periodical devoted to viniculture. Edited by George Husmann, the *Grape Culturist* featured the contributions of Missouri's prominent viticulturists, Engelmann, Bush, Muench, and Jaeger, as well as the editor. International in scope, it published correspondence, reviewed promising new grape varieties, and dispensed vineyard and winemaking advice. Each issue took readers through that month's part of the winegrowing cycle. "Friend" Husmann, as the editor was addressed, shared his ideal cellar design in a series of articles, a pattern copied by many as perfect. Due to modest advertising and subscription revenues, the *Grape Culturist* survived only three years. Yet during its life, the publication secured Husmann's already distinguished reputation in viticulture.

Following a period of time as a nurseryman in Sedalia, Husmann accepted a position at the University of Missouri, as professor of pomology (fruit growing) and forestry. During his tenure in Columbia, Husmann planted the present-day "white campus" in grape vines. The building in which he stored the vintage from this research plot became the object of infamous student raids because of Husmann's experimental wines in the basement. It was destroyed by fire in 1892. In 1881, a year after publishing his landmark work, *American Grape Growing and Wine Making*, he moved to California and joined Napa Valley's Talcoa Vineyards to enlist the wealth of his viticultural knowledge in the battle against *Phylloxera*.

DEVASTATION AND DORMANCY

Prior to the onset of Prohibition, more than one hundred wineries operated in Missouri. Hermann alone boasted at least twenty commercial-scale operations. The Augusta area contained about twelve separate wineries, vinifying grapes from the Femme Osage valley. Despite the success of the Missouri wine industry, its hoped-for destiny was nipped in the bud by the passage of the Volstead Act in 1920.

Comparable to the *Phylloxera* plague that spread across France in the previous century, the temperance movement had grown from a tiny spark to inflame the United States state by state. After decades of smoldering through the countryside, it first burst into flame as wartime Prohibition in 1919, ostensibly to reserve grain for feeding the troops. In the next year, Congress galvanized the goals of the "drys" by enacting the Volstead Prohibition Act and adopting the Eighteenth Amendment to the Constitution.

In crusading against the evils of drunkenness, the movement's militants condemned the consumption of all forms of alcohol. Their appeal was practically irresistible, as many Americans witnessed the spectacle of drunkenness on their streets or suffered its symptoms of abuse at home. Consumption of hard liquor for the purpose of becoming drunk had, through an abundance of grain in this land, become closely identified with the brash national character much as John Barleycorn characterized the English spirit of mirth. In addition, the cultural background of many American groups relegated wine to church ceremony alone, as long as the "real stuff"—corn liquor and rye whiskey—was so easily available and expedient in accomplishing its simple purpose.

As early as 1865 Friedrich Muench had addressed the concerns of a growing sentiment against the use of alcoholic beverages. In his *School for American Grape Culture*, he preached for moderation:

> There exists no moderately-cultivated people who have not added some stimulant to the simply nourishing food and drink. Thus, among ourselves, besides coffee and tea, are found the intoxicating beverages, brandy, beer and wine. It will do good to no one to use distilled liquors abundantly or in excess. . . . [W]ine surpasses all other stimulants as an enlivening, cheering, healthy drink, and, moderately used, the greatly diluted alcohol which it contains, together with the vinous acid, harmless in every respect, is recreating for the time and without any bad after effects.

Few parts of the country rejected Prohibition. Of Missouri's 114 counties, sixty-nine tallied a majority of votes for the amendment in 1915. Naturally, the dissenting counties included the winegrowing regions of Gasconade, Warren, and Washington. Those who voted against Prohibition saw the government taking food from their tables and stigmatizing a cultural practice. For many rural communities, such as Hermann, the law also crushed a profitable form of agriculture.

After the Volstead Act was passed wineries from coast to coast tore out their vineyards. Winery buildings were adapted to new uses or allowed to decay. Stone Hill converted its massive arched cellars, among the largest in the United States, into mushroom beds. Also in Hermann, the Kropp brewery and winery, reincarnated as Hermannhof Winery in recent years, became an apartment building, offering tenants ample storage in its cellars. In the state of Missouri, only the winery at St. Stanislaus Seminary in Florissant continued to operate during the 1920s, making sacramental wine for religious organizations throughout the Midwest.

Some grape growers, such as the Italians in Rosati, survived Prohibition by planting table and juice grapes in place of specialized wine-producing varieties. In fact, Prohibition and the success of the Welch's Grape Juice Company led the Rosati grape growers to increase vineyard acreage dramatically during the years of the ''noble experiment'' and to form a growers' cooperative that would eventually take over the juice firm.

CRUSADERS OF TEMPERANCE

Next to the notoriety of axe-wielding Carry Nation, the fame of Dr. Thomas B. Welch as a prohibitionist outlasted the legislation. A dentist by trade, as well as an ordained minister, Welch subscribed to the popular prohibitionist interpretation of the Bible, that the sacramental wine referred to in scripture was actually unfermented grape juice. To comply with such a stricture, temperance churches in the late nineteenth century often boiled raisins to produce nonintoxicating ''wine'' for their celebrations of the Eucharist.

Following the experiments of Louis Pasteur in France, Welch found that heating grape juice on the kitchen stove of his Vineland, New Jersey, home rendered the juice ''pure'' of alcohol-producing yeast. In 1869 ''Dr. Welch's Unfermented Wine,'' the first no-alcohol grape juice, became a staple for church altars in America and elsewhere.

Dr. Welch's son, Charles, also a dentist, realized the potential market for this product more completely than did his father. Through a media campaign that touted the medicinal benefits of the juice as much as its scriptural purity, Charles raised the annual output of the Welch's Grape Juice Company to 50,000 gallons by 1897. Fostering the development of a ''Grape Belt'' around

Lake Erie's shore in northern Pennsylvania and western New York, Welch's continued its westward expansion by building a grape processing plant in Springdale, Arkansas. As had happened in the eastern Grape Belt, Ozark vineyards became a virtual factory for supplying Concords to the Welch's Grape Juice Company. Ironically, the inventor of "Dr. Welch's Unfermented Wine" died before the enactment of Prohibition. As a further irony, the firm turned to making a low-alcohol kosher wine, "Welch's Refreshment Wine," in 1950, a quarter of a century after Charles's death.

Prohibition had immediate and long-term effects on the winemaking industry in America. Over the fourteen years of the "noble experiment," winemakers abandoned their craft for other pursuits. Carefully cultivated wine grapes, representing the toil of perhaps several generations, were uprooted. Further, wine drinkers lost their taste for fine wine as they accustomed themselves to the sweet, strong concoctions of bootleggers.

While most wineries went out of business altogether during Prohibition, those in California fared slightly better than other regions. Not a few West Coast wineries replanted their vineyards with Alicante Bouschet, a thick-skinned wine grape. In blending, this grape had previously been used to impart a deep, rich color to red wines, called *teinturier* wine. Shipping carloads of this sturdy grape eastward, California supplied the raw materials for making tinted wine to amateur winemakers. The Volstead Act excluded from penalty those who made "nonintoxicating cider and fruit juices exclusively for use in the home." Yet, given the proper ingredients, the fermentation of grape juice could have been regarded as an accident of nature. In addition, home winemakers found the Alicante Bouschet grape to be so full of color that the skins removed from the initial pressing were capable of producing a colorful second vintage by adding sugared water and yeast. California grape growers also advised consumers not to add yeast lest their juice turn into an illegal beverage.

REPEAL AND RECOVERY

In 1933, after years of political agitation, the Twenty-First amendment repealed Prohibition. To slake the thirst of their customers, merchants exhumed musty bottles from forgotten cellars. They often fortified these ancient vintages with distilled spirits to satisfy the palate of Americans who had developed a liking for white lightning and bathtub gin. Another quick-fix liquor, called "Sneaky Pete," was a popular muscatel-sherry-port vinified from Thompson seedless grapes, usually grown for snacking.

With their farms still groomed to viticulture, California winegrowers rushed to fill America's cup. The climate of California, perfectly suited to growing wine grapes, encouraged a new generation of winemakers to experiment with modern growing and processing techniques. Enology, the science of making wine, became a well-endowed curriculum in the state's agricultural schools. At the University of California at Davis, Dr. Albert Winkler devised the formula of "heat-summation" to measure the solar exposure of a grape-growing region. This information enabled growers to match their climate with the grape varieties that grew well in similar conditions.

Experiments also noted the importance of aging wine in French oak casks to achieve an added complexity of aroma and flavor. Hanzell Vineyards north of Sonoma, founded by James D. Zellerbach, a United States ambassador to Italy until 1948, cultivated Chardonnay, a grape particularly fond of the California sun and soil. Aged in French oak casks, the resulting buttery, golden wine brought world-wide attention to the state as the producer of excellent vintages. The efforts of Robert Mondavi also aided the success of California wines, as he employed precisely cooled stainless steel vats to control the fermentation process.

Proud of the success of their innovations, California wineries switched from shipping bulk tanks of their juice to bottling their vintages on site. This marketing ploy, coupled with strong, positive advertisements in the media and attractive packaging, popularized California wines throughout the United States. In the process, consumers became increasingly aware of quality, style, and varietal differences among domestic wines. Further, California wines bottled on the West Coast attracted their devotees with two advantages: consistent quality and reasonable prices.

In Missouri in 1933, few vineyards had remained intact. The St. Stanislaus Winery was officially bonded to resume commercial winemaking. Two years later, the seminary offered a port named for Bishop DuBourg and a sweet white wine named for Ste. Rose Philippine Duchesne, as well as its mainstay, De Smet Mass wine, a white.

Other Missouri vineyards at Repeal primarily grew Concord grapes for juice. In 1934 the community of Rosati had 800 acres planted in grape vines. During World War II, the Rosati vineyards, then owned by Welch's Grape Juice Company, employed captured German soldiers. At this "prison" in the heartland of America, the POWs made grape jelly for the United States military. In the mid-1950s, the Rosati grape growers' cooperative joined the National Grape Cooperative and took over the Welch's business.

Many states, including Missouri, suffered lingering effects of Prohibition for years afterward in restrictions on the availability of wine. The spirit of Prohibition stayed alive in a number of tangible ways: "dry" communities continued to prohibit the sale of packaged alcohol; punitive "sin" taxes were levied against alcoholic beverages; state liquor stores monopolized the wine market, removing it from grocery store shelves; postal laws prohibited mailing alcoholic beverages; high license fees and "occupation taxes" were required to operate a winery; and the infamous blue laws made it illegal to sell liquor on Sunday.

The French have an axiom about winemaking that might also apply to the post-Prohibition climate in America. In deference to the whims of their weather, they say adversity improves the wine. The chill of Prohibition nearly destroyed viniculture in this country. As evidenced by the California industry in the 1950s and later, however, wineries started anew, adding new knowledge and techniques to a centuries-old process steeped in tradition and mystique.

Some years after the experimental phase in California, Missouri winemakers applied similar resuscitation techniques to their state's winegrowing agriculture, searching for the grapes best suited to this climate and adopting processes for the exact monitoring of vinification. Now, positive results from their daring efforts are once again capturing the attention of wine lovers throughout the world. Missouri winemaking has returned to the threshold of its once-undisputed glory.

NEW VINES, NEW WINES

THE REVIVAL OF WINEMAKING IN MISSOURI began in the mid-1960s with the return of Hermann's Stone Hill Winery to its original purpose. In 1965, Jim and Betty Held purchased the historic site, which featured the largest vaulted cellars in the United States. For years the Helds had grown grapes on their nearby farm, selling their modest harvest to Meier's Wine Cellars in Cincinnati. Certainly the Helds realized the significance of the winery to the history of their community and state. However, they only dreamed that the winery would again become a respected contributor to winemaking in America. An even more distant possibility than restoring the vineyards was that the Helds would lead a groundswell of renewed interest in the winemaking heritage that rightfully belonged to Missouri.

About the same time that Jim and Betty Held brushed the mushrooms out of Stone Hill's cellars, the Augusta vineyards first planted by Georg Muench in 1881 bloomed again. In 1966 Lucian and Eva Dressel purchased Mt. Pleasant Winery. Under the care of the Muench family, the winery had won medals at the 1893 Columbian Exposition in Chicago and the 1904 World's Fair in St. Louis. Like Stone Hill, the vineyards and winery had suffered neglect in the years since Prohibition. With a love of wine swaying better judgement, the Dressels committed themselves to making wine at Mt. Pleasant again. Like the Helds, they pursued a vision that few in the sixties cheered with much enthusiasm. Perhaps their friends and family hoped that once the winemaking bubble had burst, these dreamers would come back to earth.

Rather than perch above the languid Missouri River satisfied with owning a niche of Missouri history, these modern-day pioneers answered the call of the vineyards and made wine. They might have expected snickering in response to their lofty aims; instead they sought and received support from an unlikely ally, the state. The state government acted boldly to encourage the growth of a renewed Missouri winegrowing agriculture. In 1978,

Governor Christopher Bond appointed a task force of agronomists and business leaders to investigate ways to promote the industry.

STATE SEAL OF APPROVAL

Under Governor Joseph Teasdale in 1980, the Missouri Wine Advisory Board officially embraced its mission to direct government activities in support of this agriculture. Legislators passed a sales tax on wine in 1984 to fund university research and the state Department of Agriculture's new Grape and Wine Program. From Southwest Missouri State University's Fruit Experiment Station in Mountain Grove, highly trained horticulturists worked hand in hand with the new vintners to determine the grape varieties best suited to Missouri's climate and topography. With money gathered from the tax, the state hired its first enologist and extension viticulturist in 1980.

Changes in Missouri law nurtured the embryonic industry as much as funds to support research. In 1980 the state assembly passed a law to allow wineries to increase their output from 75,000 gallons a year to 500,000. Other links in the shackles of Prohibition fell away when new laws permitted the wineries to serve tastes of their products and sell wine on their premises seven days a week. Such legislative initiatives indicated that the state lawmakers had become at least partly aware of the wineries' role in agriculture and tourism.

With the concerted support of various state agencies, a new generation of winemakers emerged to reclaim Missouri's lost heritage. They shared two important characteristics that sustained the rebirth of viniculture in the state: a love of fine wine and a willingness to experiment. Equally important, many of them applied useful skills from previous careers to running their wineries, such as marketing and business expertise, science and engineering. With a keen eye to the bottom line, the new winemakers tempered their fascination with the process with sound business principles.

In rebuilding their wineries, they studied the most current research in horticulture, fermentation chemistry, and filtration. Putting aside unwritten codes of winemaking, they tried and adopted new technologies. In the 1950s California winemakers had proven the value of precisely controlling fermentation temperature with cooled stainless steel tanks. Many Missouri winemakers applied this knowledge by installing state-of-the-art equipment on their premises, carefully controlling the fermentation process, and testing the wine at every stage of its development. As cooled stainless steel tanks replaced open wooden casks, modern science enhanced centuries-old rules of thumb.

A NEW GENERATION OF WINE LOVERS

The new breed of winemakers in Missouri has been eagerly welcomed by a new generation of wine lovers. From travels abroad and an appreciation of gourmet foods, consumers have gained knowledge and experience in wine. They have accepted wine as an integral component of fine dining and learned how to complement the foods they like with an equally likable glass of wine.

Much as the winemakers themselves, their fans have become entranced by the mystique of wine. In part, their curiosity about wines has been piqued by exotic names, such as Chardonnay, Semillion, and Pinot Noir. The common use of these and other varietal names came into favor after the repeal of Prohibition.

Wine aficionados began to look askance at the use of generic French place names such as Burgundy and Chablis on domestic wine, realizing that, strictly speaking, no American winery could produce *real* Burgundy, but only wine. Coupled with that fact, the popularity of varietal and proprietary names increased as American wineries proudly displayed their own distinctive label names, such as Fumé Blanc, Zinfandel, and Emerald Riesling. Likewise, educated consumers in Missouri responded to the lure of varietal names such as Cynthiana, Baco Noir, Chancellor, Seyval, and Vidal Blanc, as well as proprietary names like St. James Winery's School House White, Mt. Pleasant's Emigré Red, O'Vallon's Melange à Trois, and Hermanner Steinberg from Stone Hill.

Missourians became acquainted with the fruit of native vines at the Missouri State Fair, too. The wine-judging event in recent years has showcased the finest wine that Missouri growers have to offer. Even the judges admit that each year marks a perceptible improvement in the quality and special distinctiveness of Missouri wines. As a way to regulate the judging of the annual competition, the Missouri Department of Agriculture set boundaries of sweetness to define wine categories.

Dry wines in this system contain less than 0.5 percent residual sugar; wines in the semi-dry group measure between 0.5 and 1.5 percent; semi-sweet entrants have a residual sugar content between 1.5 and 2.5 percent; and the sweet wines show residual sugar above 2.5 percent. Two categories have been established for judging white hybrids, such as Seyval, Vidal, Vignoles, and Cayuga. Wines of these grapes are grouped either as dry, that is, with less than 0.5 percent residual sugar, or off-dry, that is, having a residual sugar content of 0.5 percent or more. While ostensibly used for judging purposes, these figures provide consumers with information about wine that is more descriptive than words alone.

AMERICA'S FIRST WINE DISTRICT

The turning point in the renaissance of Missouri winemaking occurred in 1980. To the surprise of many Americans, Augusta became the nation's first official viticultural area recognized by the Bureau of Alcohol, Tobacco and Firearms, a unit of the U. S. Treasury Department. In the next seven years three other Missouri winegrowing regions received a comparable designation: Hermann in 1983; the Ozark Mountains area, which includes parts of Arkansas and Oklahoma as well as southwestern Missouri, in 1986; and the Ozark Highlands region, which encompasses the south central upland prairie around St. James, in 1987. While many viticultural areas in California, Ohio, and New York have been similarly honored, Augusta, Missouri, proudly achieved this special status first.

As an American adaptation of the French *Appellation d'Origine Contrôlée*, the designation of a viticultural area takes into account a region's unique soil, climate, and winemaking history. However, the similarity between the two labeling standards ends there. Instituted in the first decades of the twentieth century, the French designation requires wines bearing a place name, such as Champagne or Burgundy, to be produced from specific grape varieties grown within the named region. For example, only winemakers in the Champagne district can legally label their wines as Champagne; others who produced this effervescent beverage had to call their product sparkling wine or ''méthode champenois,'' meaning in the style of Champagne. In addition to grape varieties, the French law also specified other attributes of wine grown in the named region, such as alcohol content, the amount of wine produced per acre, and growing and vinifying methods.

In America, wineries using the name of a viticultural area guarantee that eighty-five percent of the wine comes from grapes grown within the boundaries of the designated region. Similarly, seventy-five percent of the grapes must be of the variety named on the label if the winery chooses to use a grape name such as Cynthiana, Vignoles, or Seyval. By contrast, only fifty-one percent of a *labrusca* (Concord and Catawba) or muscadine wine must be vinified from either of these varieties to bear the grape's name.

When the Bureau of Alcohol, Tobacco and Firearms first proposed a viticultural area labeling standard for winegrowing localities in the United States, it sought regions with unique soil and topography, along with a history of winemaking. To Augusta vintners, other factors loomed even larger in the success of making wine than the badge of the federal government. Their earliest efforts to revive winegrowing in Missouri were favored by a deep layer of loess soil, warm air currents circulating through the Missouri River valley, and the protection against frigid blasts afforded by the Osage Ridge.

WINE WITH ETHNIC ROOTS

Across the state the revival of Missouri's winemaking industry has been inextricably linked with a fervor for the expression of ethnic identity. The landscape along the Missouri River valley, reminiscent of the Rhineland, distinctively shapes this ''cultural rebound,'' as German communities celebrate their ethnic roots. The city of Hermann, for example, has created a number of public celebrations around their heritage, attracting tourists from states throughout the Midwest. Where once many visitors to the Missouri countryside longed only for fishing, boating, and camping activities, they now find new points of interest. In the Ozarks and along the great rivers of the state, adventurers find winemaking as a part of historical observances, craft fairs, and ethnic festivals.

The growth of the winemaking industry can be measured in tally-sheet figures. A clear call to prospective winemakers came in 1972. In that year, Americans drank 340 million gallons of wine, a per capita rate that tripled the best year before Prohibition. Eight years later Americans consumed more wine than distilled spirits for the first time in the nation's history. In Missouri, wine lovers drank about six million gallons of wine in 1980, producing nearly $2 million in state taxes.

STIRRINGS IN THE VINEYARDS

Missouri viticulturists have enthusiastically answered the demand for premium domestic wines. Between 1982 and 1987, total acreage of wine grapes in Missouri increased nearly thirty percent. This growth shows some interesting trends. For example, the acreage for Catawba and Concord grapes (still Missouri's leading vineyard grapes) has declined, while plantings of cold-hardy Delaware and Cynthiana/Norton have more than quintupled.

The willingness to experiment also shows up in the acreage figures for hybrid varieties. Vignoles, for example, a vigorous and prolific vine, has replaced Villard Blanc vines, which were found to be particularly susceptible to crown gall. Acreages of Seyval and Vidal grapes are also expanding as these white wines prove themselves worthy of world competition. In red hybrid plantings, less dramatic growth is reflected. In the decline of Chelois and Villard Noir, plantings of Chambourcin, de Chaunac, and Chancellor vines have increased. Again, the tendency of these plants to suffer the effects of crown gall threatens to limit their acreage in Missouri.

Along with Missouri, other regions also have shaken off the sleep of Prohibition. In the past two decades, vigorous vineyard planting has spread from Thomas Jefferson's Virginia to the Finger Lakes in New York to the Willamette Valley of Oregon. Despite this renewed interest, nearly all existing literature that condescends to discuss non-Californian American wine does so disparagingly, briefly, and even nostalgically.

The stirrings in the vineyards suggest a period of experimentation for American winegrowers. Just as vintners in California set out in the years after Prohibition to cultivate the grape varieties that responded well to their climate and soil conditions, Missouri winegrowers have reestablished their vineyards in the same trial-and-error method. However, significant differences exist between the two states. First, Missouri winegrowers can benefit from California's failures and research. Second, and perhaps more important, Missouri offers potential winegrowers suitable acreage that, relative to California prices, can be purchased with a reasonable investment of capital. Finally, Missouri winegrowers can take advantage of their state's location in the heartland of the country. Major cities, such as Chicago, Dallas, Milwaukee, and Minneapolis-St. Paul, are within 500 miles of the state's borders.

Like the pioneers who followed the currents of America's waterways to arrive in the heartland, like the entrepreneurs who sponsored expeditions to the New West from the ''Gateway City,'' Missouri winemakers and wine lovers are discovering many unique advantages to this state.

WINE
TOURS

AUGUSTA

IN 1804 MERIWETHER LEWIS AND WILLIAM CLARK set out from St. Louis to explore the Louisiana Purchase. By boat they followed the Missouri River west as commissioned by Thomas Jefferson and Congress to find access to the Pacific Ocean. In memory of their expedition, the federal government in 1964 approved the designation of 3,700 miles of their route as the Lewis and Clark Trail.

From the Weldon Spring exit of Interstate 64 (Highway 40) west of St. Louis, Highway 94 follows the north bank of Lewis and Clark's river. It passes through Defiance, near the home of Daniel Boone's family where the great Cumberland pioneer died.

The rollercoaster road brushes the former track bed of the Missouri, Kansas & Texas (Katy) railroad at several access points. The juxtaposition of the erratic highway with the straight, purposeful track bed provides an odd contrast. In recent years the tracks have been removed and the bed smoothly graveled to form the Katy Trail. Today bicycling enthusiasts and hikers can begin their westward trek at Weldon Spring. The stalwart among them will arrive at Augusta at day's end, passing in the course of some fifteen miles into the nineteenth century.

At first the people of Augusta, Missouri, called their community Mount Pleasant. The name aptly described the southward view from the ridges overlooking the wide Missouri River valley. When they found out that a town in southwestern Lawrence County had already claimed this name, they adopted the name of the mayor's wife for their community. Augusta was a river town then, some fifty miles upstream from St. Louis. In the flood of 1872, the Missouri river jumped its channel at the foot of Augusta's bluffs. As the deluge subsided, the river chose a course on the other side of the valley. Augusta was no longer a river town.

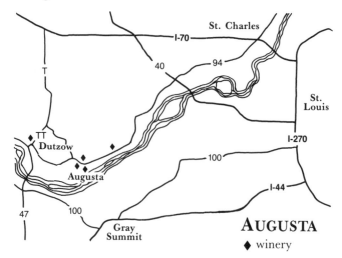

AUGUSTA
♦ winery

Augusta has remained over the last century as if preserved in a time capsule. The town exudes quaintness. Far from affected, however, its charm is genuine; the names of several leading families of a hundred years ago are still prominent: Mallinckrodt, Fuhr, and Nahm. It's almost as if the change in the river's bed stranded these families on an island a hundred years ago.

Thousands of years before the area's habitation, glaciers crept south, pushing rich topsoil ahead of its advance like folds in a tablecloth and forming the hills north of the Missouri River. The glacier left its imprint in other features that distinguish the north bank of the Missouri River by collecting a rich layer of loess soil and by scraping flat the river valley to the south. These features make the land perfect for viticulture. The sloping hillsides provide efficient air and water drainage. Facing south, they receive the warmth of the sun crossing low in the winter sky and are protected by the surrounding ridges from blasts of freezing Canadian air. The flat river valley traps the heat of the day, lapping waves of warm air currents against the slopes. When the mercury drops to below freezing in the winter, the Augusta region stays appreciably warmer. Barely noticeable to human inhabitants, the difference is significant to grape vines.

For these unique geologic features, as well as for its rich tradition as a winegrowing region—about a dozen wineries operated here before Prohibition—the federal government bestowed on Augusta the nation's first viticultural area designation in 1980. Similar to the French *Appellation d'Origine Contrôlée*, which regulates the use of place names on wine grown in renowned viticultural districts, the Augusta appellation of origin applies to a strictly defined corner of west St. Charles County, bordered by the Missouri River on the south and the Osage Ridge to the north. In the 1970s the late Clayton Byers, founder of Montelle Winery, and Lucian Dressel, who revived the Mt. Pleasant Wine Company in 1965, contemplated applying to the French government for recognition of Augusta as a distinct winegrowing area. As a former French territory, they reasoned, the area qualified for this distinction. Before they could follow through on their scheme, however, the United States Bureau of Alcohol, Tobacco and Firearms proposed its own labeling standard.

Montelle Winery

Highway 94
P.O. Box 147
Augusta MO 63332   (314) 228-4464

Ask the current proprietors of Montelle Winery to describe the most distinctive attribute of their winery and they will point to the view.

On the rim of the southeastern end of the crescent-shaped Osage Ridge, Montelle Winery perches about four hundred feet above the broad Missouri River Valley below. Two miles east of Augusta on Route 94, the winery looks out on the patchwork fields of the valley below, the thin strand of the Missouri River miles away, and the wooded vertebrae of the Osage Ridge, which curls around like the spine of a cat dozing in the sun.

Cats at Montelle Winery have lent their names to several of the thirty-four wines made there. Two of the felines, Miss Kitty and Juliet, are presently resident, unimpressed by the view, untroubled by the many visitors.

As much as to taste the wines, people come to enjoy a picnic at one of the tables that circle the winery. In addition, the "Dinner on the Ridge" gatherings sponsored by Montelle nearly every Saturday night through the summer months sell out long in advance.

Founded in 1970 by the late Clayton Byers, formerly a public relations executive in St. Louis, and his wife Nissel, Montelle Winery began life on the side of Augusta opposite its current overlook. In 1987, soon after Byers' death, Montelle merged with the Osage Ridge Winery and moved to its present location. By that time, the Byers family had been joined by Judy and Bob Slifer and Bill and Joanne Fitch.

The winery still vinifies grapes from its first location, as well as from other vineyards: Coyote Crossing, Kessler, and McNamara vineyards. The latter was the original site of Alfred Nahm's pre-Prohibition winery. In addition to these ties to Montelle's past, the Slifer and Fitch families continue to operate the winery as a living memorial to its founder, one of the key figures in the renaissance of Missouri winemaking. As much as making

French-style wine, Clayton Byers had a passion for cultivating flowers. Both are still to be found in abundance at the Montelle Winery.

Judy and Bob Slifer acquired their love and knowledge of French-style wine during a two-year assignment in Antwerp, Belgium, when Bob worked as an operations manager for Monsanto Chemical Company. They describe French-style wines as blended, aged in small oak barrels, and uncompromisingly dry. Some of their popular blends include Founder's Reserve White, the semi-dry River Country White, the dry red Reserve du Mont, and the semi-dry Spaghetti Red. They also offer fine varietal wines. From the wine competition at the 1990 Missouri State Fair, Montelle brought home gold medals for its 1989 Vignoles and its 1989 Vidal Blanc. Both wines embody the very definition of dry by containing hardly a trace of residual sugar. Montelle also won a silver medal for its 1986 Cynthiana.

For wine lovers with a palate for dessert wines, Montelle offers several sweet blends, including Gloria, Augustaner, and Sweet Briar. Three fruit wines are also available—Blackberry, Red Raspberry, and Golden Gooseberry. For a cool refreshment without alcohol on a hot summer day, the winery has both carbonated and noncarbonated grape juices. Visitors may take a free tour and taste Montelle wines every day of the week. Cheese and sausage plates can be assembled from the winery's cooler for a picnic on the ridge. Cats are available on a finicky basis for petting.

Mount Pleasant Vineyards

5634 High Street
Augusta MO 63332   (314) 228-4419

Less than two miles farther west on Route 94, the sharp-spired Christ Lutheran Church welcomes travelers to Augusta. Along narrow village streets better suited to a buggy than the horseless carriage, well-placed signs point the way to Mt. Pleasant Wine Company. Using the original cellar and buildings built in 1881 by Georg Muench, Mt. Pleasant returned to the world of winemaking in 1965 through the vision of Eva and Lucian Dressel. Pioneers in what many considered a losing cause, these two have continued to face forward while maintaining the winery's ties to the past.

They, like Augusta winemakers of the previous century, believe in taking risks. Viticulture, perhaps more than any other form of agriculture, requires much capital and labor. From the deck of a modern, glass-enclosed lodge, complete with air conditioning, Lucian surveys rows of Chardonnay on the south-facing slopes below. He is adamant: in *vinifera* and European-style wines lies the future of Missouri winemaking. Without a trace of trepidation, he acknowledges that he is among three people in the state who might allow that the fragile vines of Europe stand a chance in the wilds of Missouri. When pressed further, he admits that the other two people possibly sharing this view are Eva and their son Fred.

Over the past twenty-five years, they have expanded plantings to the point where Chardonnay now outproduces either Seyval or Vidal in the Mt. Pleasant vineyards. In addition, all European grape plantings combine to surpass total French-American hybrid acreage.

Lucian calculates that growing these varieties takes two to three times more care than hybrid or native American grapes. Each of the Chardonnay vines over the edge of the deck is accompanied by a substantial post in the ground. To prepare for winter the plants are individually jacketed in straw and fenced. Even with that layer of protection, these delicate vines require the best vineyard site to survive winter temperatures that can dip well below zero for days.

Skeptics scoff at the Dressels' brash determination; still crazy after all these years, the sympathetic might sigh. Yet Mt. Pleasant hauls home awards by the barrel. In Lucian's view, these contests, particularly international gatherings, demonstrate a winery's performance over time and identify for the consumer the contending players in the world of wine; and the Dressels' continuing goal has been to compete worldwide.

Now a solidly middle-aged man—he regrets that no one any longer asks why a youngster such as himself goes into such a risky endeavor—Lucian has had an intimation of immortality. "I don't want to grow old and die having only created a successful regional wine, having passed my life in building a quaint *Weinstube* in the hinterland," he says. "Instead, I am compelled to enter contests where the ground rules and the benchmark have been established according to the standards of quality defined by the world.''

As we say in Missouri, ''The proof of the pudding is in the eating.'' During the Muench family's tenure on this property, the winery began its record of success with awards at the 1893 World's Columbian Exposition in Chicago and the 1904 Louisiana Purchase Exposition in St. Louis. More to the present, Mt. Pleasant won seven medals, including four gold, in the 1990 Missouri State Fair. In fact, the winery claims the most awards of any Missouri winery.

Lucian concludes his ''medal spiel'' saying that he is inclined to dote a bit on the silver medal for his 1986 Vintage Port that he brought home from the International Wine and Spirits Competition in London in 1989 and the gold medal for his 1986 Brut Champagne from the Eastern International Wine Competition in New York in 1989.

As an interesting footnote about Mt. Pleasant's Vintage Port, Lucian explains that he obtained the recipe, as well as vine cuttings, for this award-winning libation from the Jesuits at St. Stanislaus. The St. Louis County seminary had grown and made wine from around 1823 to 1960 without interruption. When the order decided to sell the campus, their vineyards and expertise might have been found only in history books but for the interest of Lucian Dressel.

In the closing days of St. Stanislaus Seminary, Brother Lawrence Eilert, the seminary's last winemaker, divulged his secrets to Lucian. He made only one request in exchange: that Mt. Pleasant wines made from the St. Stanislaus recipe should tell the story of the seminary on their labels. Among other vintages, Mt. Pleasant's Cordon Rouge of 1979 memorialized the hard work of the St. Stanislaus winegrowers. In a botanical sense, the vines of St. Stanislaus still bear wine on the hillsides of Augusta.

In addition to the wines, history, and scenery of Mt. Pleasant, visitors enjoy Missouri sausages and cheeses on the deck or in the lodge. These items, as well as many unique crafts and souvenirs, are offered by Eva Dressel at the Cheese Wedge in one of the winery's nineteenth-century buildings. The winery is open for free tours and wine tasting seven days a week, except major holidays.

Augusta Winery

P.O. Box 8
Augusta MO 63332   (314) 228-4301

In the years before the Missouri River slipped across the valley from Augusta, steamboat passengers disembarked at the foot of Jackson Street. A selection of hotels greeted them. Farther into town, the intersection of Jackson and High streets marked the hub of commerce in Augusta. Following in the footsteps of nineteenth century adventurers, modern-day cyclists on the Katy Trail climb the hill from the former railroad track bed. On the northwest corner of Jackson and High streets now stands a redwood, glass, and flagstone structure, a sleek upstart among old brick and clapboard neighbors. Its very presence here is a surprise, a dislocation of time and place that hints of further surprises inside the Augusta Winery.

The only obvious link that ties the Augusta Winery to the past is its wine. With several wines made exclusively from grapes grown within the viticultural area, the wines embody a style that is becoming recognized as unique to the region as Burgundy is to its namesake province in France. The proprietor, Tony Kooyumjian, has been making wine for ten years. He opened Augusta Winery in the spring of 1990; in that summer three wines from the current list of six won medals at the Missouri State Fair. A fourth wine brought home a medal from the International Eastern Wine Competition in New York. Upstart, indeed!

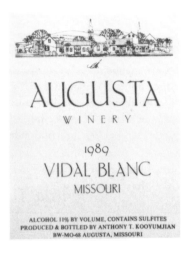

Tony has definite goals for the Augusta Winery: to make high quality, little-processed wine from grapes grown only by conscientious growers; to ensure quality by selling the wines only in the tasting room; and to maintain direct contact with customers. Tony labels the growers he chooses as ''progressive''— experts at growing wine grapes in particular. By obtaining the harvest of such growers, Tony knows his use of preservatives and anti-oxidants to stabilize the wine will be minimal. This confidence in his growers gives him the freedom to exercise his skill as a winemaker.

By selling the wines only through the tasting room, Tony can assure his customers that each bottle has been properly and considerately handled. This means that Tony will not have to process the wine with the idea of shipment in mind. Some wines from far-distant points employ chemical stabilizers to assure the buyer of consistent quality. Comparable to supermarket tomatoes, those wines are harvested hard and pale, lacking that lush, home-grown flavor. Tony's marketing technique also provides him and his staff with customer contact. They can hear for themselves how the wines are received, whether the winemaker has hit the mark in this blend or with that varietal. The exchange of information at the tasting counter travels two ways. The Augusta Winery staff can assist wine lovers with information about growing and processing conditions, recommendations to satisfy any palate, and recipes that call for wine.

While all the processing of the grapes takes place at the winery, no tours are available on a regular basis. Instead, the visitor to the Augusta Winery is invited to taste the wines and enjoy some easy moments of conviviality at wrought-iron tables in the spacious skylighted tasting room, appointed with the artwork of John Pils, or on the terrace next to the passing humanity on Jackson Street. Cheese and sausage plates are also available.

The Augusta Winery has proved its mettle and its right to an honored place at the table with other, long-established wineries by earning medals at the 1990 Missouri State Fair for its off-dry Seyval; its Augusta Blush, a blend of Villard Noir and Steuben grapes; and its Augusta White, a late harvest Seyval. All three bear the owl seal earned only by wines grown and vinted in the Augusta viticultural area. The White Reserve, meanwhile, placed at the International Eastern Wine Competition in New York. Another wine of note, the Red Reserve, combines Chancellor Noir and Cynthiana grapes that, through aging in Missouri oak barrels, develops hints of wild cherry and vanilla with a tang of bell pepper. The crisp Vidal Blanc, aged in small oak cooperage and with a lingering flavor, rounds out the wine list of the Augusta Winery. (Long-finish, or lingering flavor is preferable to an after-taste.)

Black Horse Winery

274 Jackson Street
Augusta MO 65233   (314) 228-4404

Directly across Jackson Street from the Augusta Winery

is another upstart, Black Horse Winery. Its owners, a group of people with a taste for fine wine and show horses, might have intended to suggest a double meaning by the winery's name. As the newest arrival to the village of Augusta, the winery is a dark horse among the pedigreed.

The grapes that go into Black Horse wines, grown exclusively in the Augusta viticultural area, come from vineyards that have been under cultivation for the past decade. In 1990, its first year of operation, the winery produced eight wines, all of the 1989 vintage, ranging from dry to sweet. In varietal wine, the winery offers a Seyval Blanc, a Vidal Blanc, and a Villard Noir. Blends include Missouri Rhineland, made principally from Missouri Riesling grapes, the Derby Blush, the White Labrusca, and the Red Labrusca. Four medals at the 1990 International Eastern Wine Competition in New York went to the Black Horse Winery's first releases, including a first place finish for the 1989 Norton. Due to the winery's small size, however, and the winemaker's insistence on crafting small amounts of handmade wine, the popular selections quickly sell out.

While no tour as such is offered, the tasting room at the corner of High and Jackson streets serves samples of the remaining selection of wines.

Blumenhof Vineyards & Winery

Highway 94
P. O. Box 30
Dutzow MO 63342   (314) 443-2245

Seven miles west of Augusta on Route 94, the Blumenhof Winery rests confidently at the edge of the Augusta viticultural area. The boundary described by the Bureau of Alcohol, Tobacco and Firearms falls at the Warren County line just short of Blumenhof. Nonetheless, James Blumenberg, patriarch of the family that operates the winery, feels no disadvantage at this. He claims growing conditions west of the viticultural area surpass those of Augusta, as he describes its geologic and climatic features.

Blumenhof Winery is a family operation in the tradition of the estates of Europe. Son Mark and daughter-in-law Linda tend thirteen acres of French-American hybrids near the winery. Built into the side of a hill, a Swiss-style chalet greets visitors with the old-world charm of the Blumenberg family's origins in the Harz Mountains of Germany. The tasting room deck looks out on a cool, quiet country dell. More than any other winery, this location is Duden country. Gottfried Duden, the vanguard of German emigration to Missouri in the first half of the nineteenth century, lived not a mile down the road. Much of his love affair with Missouri, published and widely distributed in Germany in the 1830s, was based on his jaunts through this countryside.

Among the followers of Duden, Baron von Bock led a party of freedom-loving Germans to these hills north of the Missouri River to found the town of Dutzow in 1832. Friedrich Muench also chose farmland near the Blumenhof Winery as his home. In 1881, with pruning shears in hand, Muench died as he had wished, tending his beloved vines at his farm.

The Blumenbergs carry on the viticultural tradition of Muench with respect for the region's history. Though nearly all of their vineyard acreage is planted in hybrids that did not exist in the time of Muench, they also cultivate Cynthiana, a native American variety that

Muench proclaimed to be the equal of any red grape in the world for making fine red wine. Evidence of the truth of this conviction came to Blumenhof Winery when its 1988 Cynthiana won first place at the Florida State Fair in 1989 and a bronze medal at the prestigious InterVin international wine competition held in New York in 1990.

Though the winery released its first wine only in 1987, a steady stream of awards has vaulted Blumenhof wines to the forefront of the renaissance of winemaking in Missouri. Its 1987 Vintage Reserve Vidal Blanc, for example, garnered gold medals at the Missouri State Fair and the International Eastern Wine Competition in 1988. Similarly, its off-dry 1988 Vintage Reserve Vidal Blanc wears medals from the 1989 competition in New York and the 1990 Missouri State Fair. Releases of the winery's Cayuga White have also been steady performers on the competition circuit. Referred to as the ''Riesling of the East,'' Cayuga was developed from Seyval and *Vitis labrusca* parents at the State Agricultural Experiment Station in Geneva, New York.

For its red wines and Vidal, Blumenhof uses French oak and American oak cooperage. The differences in the two woods go beyond cost in their effect on the winemaker's craft. Dense French oak barrels impart a lingering hint of wood to well-made wines; its American cousin, meanwhile, more open grained than the French, tends toward a bluntness, like the character of the people who tamed this land. Jim Blumenberg cautions that any oak cooperage can be unpredictable; with too much time in American oak in particular, the delicate flavors and aroma of fine wine can be overpowered by the effects of the wood. At the same time, Jim notes the pleasure of discovering a wine as if for the first time when, after bottling, it has matured through a brash and possibly discordant youth into a wine of subtle complexity and mellowness.

All the variables that go into growing and making wine seem to have come up roses at the Blumenhof Winery. True to the winery's name, translated as "Court of Flowers," blossoms line the concrete ramp to the tasting room. Visitors are invited to sample the Blumenhof wines, picnic on the deck or in the shaded dell, and arrange a winery tour, seven days a week.

HERMANN

For years in many American cities, archi-tects and urban planners sold a sleek, featureless style as progress. They pushed aside old structures and old-fashioned values for the latest convenience. At best, a building or two survived the headache ball and the compulsion to modernize. Often relegated to the role of museums, these relics stood apart as tombstones for a previous life—dried flowers among stainless steel and concrete. Like many other towns in this country today, however, Hermann has made a commitment to preserve and nurture its past.

In fact, the community traces its beginning to that same ideal. In 1837 members of the German Settlement Society of Philadelphia came west in search of a place where they could preserve their German culture. Ever since that time the town has held fast to its heritage. Although the German language no longer expresses the voice of commerce or the lessons of school children, Her-mann still is German.

Hugging the south bank of the Missouri River, the city of Hermann has grown over the hills where acres of vines once thrived. Market Street, originally laid out to be wider than any street in Philadelphia of the 1830s, bisects the town north and south and absorbs traffic from the sixty-year-old bridge that brings Highway 19 across the river to merge with Highway 100. The restaurants, lodgings, and shops that line this thoroughfare reflect the German character of the town as much as the parallel avenues Goethe, Mozart, Schiller, and Gutenberg.

Perpendicular to Market Street, First Street to the east leads to the landing that welcomed steamboats full of visitors from St. Louis in the last century. Now the Union Pacific Railroad tracks trace the winding course of the river; freight and passenger trains barrel through town without stopping, except for two times each year. During one weekend in May and every weekend in October,

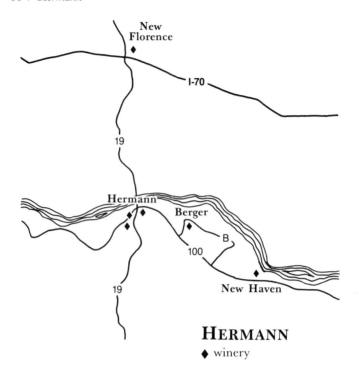

HERMANN
♦ winery

special Amtrak cars bring tourists to revel in festivities that display the German character of Hermann. For these celebrations, bratwurst sizzles on open-air grills in *Biergärten* throughout the city, polka bands exhort couples to dance, and boys in *Lederhosen* execute a foot-stomping, leather-slapping precision drill as *Mädchen* in lace petticoats twirl in waltz time. Some of the spectators sport buttons that say, "Kiss me, I'm German"; others wade through the throng in T-shirts emblazoned with "I survived the Oktoberfest."

Outside of the Maifest and Oktoberfest, the tranquility of a rural American town returns to Hermann, in many ways typical of towns in the Midwest. It has its Ford dealership, its pizza parlor, its drugstore, its taverns, and its main-street cafes. Crossing the bridge from the north or following the Highway 100 river route, visitors to Hermann might perceive one enormous difference as they approach the city limits: Hermann, the home of as many as sixty wineries before Prohibition, also has its wineries today.

Stone Hill Winery

Highway 19
Rt. 1, Box 26
Hermann MO 65041   (314) 486-2221

Longtime residents of Hermann identify each other by branches on a family tree. In a sense, the commitment of Jim and Betty Held, the proprietors of the Stone Hill Wine Company, directly connects them to the winery's founder, Michael Poeschel. The Helds revived the winery in 1965, years after Prohibition had condemned its massive cellars to growing mushrooms.

Poeschel had begun the winery modestly enough in 1847, taking John Scherer as a partner in 1861. Later, the firm expanded to include William Herzog and George Stark. At the 1873 World Exposition in Vienna, this winery from the heart of Missouri began its distinguished record of winning international awards. Over the next thirty years, Stone Hill Wine Company won gold medals at eight world fairs, including the "Grand Medal" at the 1904 Louisiana Purchase Exposition in St. Louis.

Jim Held talks nostalgically about Stone Hill's past. He believes that the winery's Red Label Burgundy and Norton won many nineteenth-century awards. In a wistful tone, he points out that these ribbons now rest in the German School Museum in town. He feels that these trophies, part of Stone Hill's past, belong with the many ribbons Stone Hill has won since 1965.

Nonetheless, when he and Betty revived Stone Hill, they inherited much more history than the ribbons alone can suggest. In addition to a few Norton vines planted immediately after the Civil War, the winery, before Prohibition the second largest in the United States, included cellars and buildings built by the founder and his partners. Legends, like the remembrance of yesterday's wine, linger and take on a life of their own. The apostle casks, for instance, once occupied the arched openings in the winery's main cellar. Each of the twelve 1,500 to 2,000-gallon barrels bore an ornate carving of one of the twelve disciples of Christ. At the outbreak of Prohibition, these works of art were gingerly dismantled, carefully packed, and shipped east with a final destination of Germany. From the shipping invoice, the trail of these relics vanishes like train tracks absorbed by the horizon. Not even a picture remains to attest to their grandeur.

These days, the Helds have done more for the renaissance of winemaking in Missouri than simply restoring Stone Hill's landmark structures. They also cultivate several kinds of grapes from sixty acres on hilltops south of town, including Norton's Virginia Seedling planted on the old Rausch homestead at the end of the Civil War. The elevation of these plots, Jim says, favors the land for winegrowing by promoting cold-air flow to the valleys below. The mainly northern exposure also provides a more consistent temperature for the vineyard than slopes that receive winter sun directly.

Jim and Betty Held look forward to passing this heritage on to the next generation. What does it mean to Jim that three of his children have become involved in the business? "It means everything," he simply and unequivocally states. Daughter Patty and son Jon, both graduates of the California State University at Fresno, apply their skills and experience to the Stone Hill Wine Company in Hermann. Thomas Held, who like his siblings studied enology and viticulture at Fresno, graduated with a degree in food sciences from the University of Arkansas in Fayetteville and operates the family's Branson branch, Stone Hill III.

For the last twelve years, the Held family's commitment to Stone Hill has been complemented by the winemaking expertise of Dave Johnson. The awards earned by this combination of talent are impressive. Even though an array of medallions and ribbons from state, national, and international competitions festoon the Stone Hill tasting room, the winery's staff take at least an equal amount of satisfaction in comments from the public.

Their tasting menu begins with the dry, complex Norton, which promises a delightful surprise to those who can cellar the 1987 vintage for five to ten years. In dry white wines, Stone Hill's 1989 Vidal won medals at the San Francisco Fair and the Missouri State Fair. Two types

STONE HILL

1987
ESTATE BOTTLED HERMANN
Norton

PRODUCED AND BOTTLED BY STONE HILL WINERY
In The Hills Of HERMANN, MO. Alcohol 12% By Volume

of Seyval, one version fermented in oak barrels, have won national and international awards, as well as honors at the 1990 Missouri State Fair. Its off-dry 1989 Vignoles, which, to Jim Held represents perhaps the most promising future for Missouri winemaking, has similarly been recognized at national and international wine tasting venues. To the winery's loyal fans, the German-style Hermanner Steinberg continues to be a favorite white, along with the red Beaujolais-like Hermannsberger. Its Missouri Champagne, Golden Spumante, and Spumante Blush, all made at Stone Hill II in New Florence (see below), offer those who appreciate sparkling wines, or simply need to christen a boat, beverages to highlight special occasions. It was a bottle of Stone Hill champagne, after all, that launched the original battleship *Missouri* in 1901.

The winery's tasting room and gift shop are free and open to the public. For a nominal fee, visitors may take a guided tour through the cellars of Stone Hill. As a simply relaxing afternoon, wine lovers can purchase a bottle of wine, a wedge of cheese, and a link of sausage, and enjoy the spectacular view of the spires of Hermann churches and the Missouri River valley.

Adam Puchta & Son Winery

Rt. 1, Box 73
Frene Creek County Road
Hermann MO 65041   (314) 486-2361

As the sixth generation of his family to make wine, Tim Puchta accepted an enormous responsibility in continuing this tradition. At the Puchta family farm south of Hermann on Frene Creek County Road, a gravel branch off Highway 100, the winery started by Adam Puchta in 1855 had not operated since the onset of Prohibition. Like a forest, the Puchtas' history covers Frene Creek Valley, a history all but forgotten to those outside of the immediate family. The tranquility of the landscape begs to be left alone. Yet Tim Puchta's father was born here, his grandfather and great-grandfather, too. He does not want to betray the beauty of nature; at the same time, he cannot ignore his family's heritage and ties with this land.

John Henry Puchta came to Hermann with the German Settlement Society of Philadelphia in the 1830s, his young son Adam in tow. The family hailed from Bavaria. In 1853 gold fever struck Adam. While the young man probably did not strike it rich during his nearly three-year stay in California, he earned enough money to return to Hermann and build a winery on land adjacent to his father's home. In 1855 Adam built the cellar, a forty-foot-long arched crypt. He used the most readily available materials throughout. Whereas most cellars from the nineteenth century incorporate manufactured bricks for the arched ceiling, the Puchta cellar uses rough-hewn stone, painstakingly cut to form the fifteen-foot-high vault. With timbers felled from the property, Adam built a barn on top of his cellar. In 1858 he upgraded his farm with a two-story rock house next to the cellar. Divided by a center hall, the first floor of the house had two large rooms. Hired help stayed in the attic above the family's main-floor quarters. A root cellar under one half of the house stored the family's winter provisions.

Adam Puchta first married Clementina Riefensthal, the elder daughter of George Riefensthal, one of the original settlers of Hermann and the winegrower who delivered cuttings of Norton's Virginia Seedling into the hands of Jacob Rommel. Clementina died shortly after the death of their first-born child, an infant daughter. Later, Adam Puchta married the younger Riefensthal daughter, Bertha, the first girl born in the colony of Hermann. From this marriage was born Henry Adam Puchta, Tim Puchta's great-grandfather.

ADAM PUCHTA

1989
Adam's Choice
MISSOURI WHITE WINE

Produced and Bottled by Adam Puchta, Inc.,
Hermann, Mo.   Alcohol 11% By Volume
Contains Sulfites

Tim wrestles with the enormous task of restoring the Adam Puchta & Son winery. "This place is so peaceful," he says as a breeze lightly stirs the trees, "I don't want that to change by opening up the winery again." Yet he found the cellar virtually intact; it now houses stainless-steel vats where fermenting Seyval and Chambourcin bubble away. He sketches a word picture of how the place will be: The barn above the cellar will contain the winemaking facility, where Adam's wine press and crusher now rest; the rock house next door will become the tasting room, surrounded on two sides by a brick patio; and rows of vines will line the hillsides overlooking the winery and Frene Creek Valley.

One of Tim's goals is to establish a vineyard of Cynthiana and Norton, planted side by side. With these two plants growing under nearly identical soil and climatic conditions, separately vinified varietals will contribute

substantial evidence to the debate over the differences
between the plants. Like other Missouri winemakers Tim
sees a promising future for Vignoles, a hybrid developed
in France.

Even though the finishing strokes will not be applied
for several years, Tim and his wife, Vicki, welcomed the
public to their peaceful valley in October of 1990. To
achieve this end, they labored along with Tim's father,
Judge Randolph Puchta. As a brother bulldozed a park-
ing lot into the hillside, Tim and Vicki's newborn son
observed all the action from his swing. The boy has yet
to learn about the proud history of the Puchta family,
has yet to don the mantle of the seventh generation to
live here, has yet to hear the call of the vineyard.

Hermannhof Vineyards

330 E. First Street
Hermann MO 65041   (314) 486-5959

Beginning its life as the Kropp Brewery in 1852, Hermannhof resurfaced as a winery in 1978 due to the efforts of Jim Dierberg, president of First Bank. This
historic building, located on the eastern approach to Hermann, had already been converted to apartments when
Prohibition ended the life of Hugo Kropp's brewery and
tavern in 1920. In the decades that followed, residents
used the vents leading to the cellars as trash receptacles.
Jim's first dream of establishing a winery there might
have been dampened by the pails of garbage that had
to be excavated from the underground vaults, but the
task was rewarded by the magnificent wine cellars that
emerged.

Underneath the Hermannhof tasting room and dining room, arched cellars form a network of connecting
rooms. Damp with underground seepage, the cellars are
atop smooth bedrock. Geologists have determined that
eons ago this was the northern shore of the Gulf of Mex-
ico. Al Marks, Hermannhof's winemaker, admits that
the damp conditions do not help his craft. Yet the eerie
isolation of the caverns sets the perfect scene to perform

the magic of vinifying grapes.

Al Marks's particular style of magic relies heavily on Old World techniques for making wine. While he does not arbitrarily cast aside the tools and knowledge of modern science, he studies how traditional winemaking procedures can enhance the accepted practices of the current age. For example, Al believes that the use of sulfites to preserve wine can be minimal by letting the oxidizing components that cause wine to brown settle out. He has also applied the Old World practice of carbonic maceration to Chambourcin grapes. In this technique, whole bunches of grapes, including some stems, are loaded into a stainless-steel fermentation tank. The sheer weight of the grapes splits the skins, allowing the yeast to enter the grapes in its quest for sugar. Thus, much of the fermentation takes place inside the grapes. Later, the juice is separated from the solid matter, while the wine typically retains the freshness of fruit and lightness of a Beaujolais nouveau.

Currently president of the Missouri Vintners' Association, Al has specialized in the study of wines of the Midwest. Originally from St. Louis, Al studied enology and viticulture at the University of Arkansas in Fayetteville, perhaps the Midwest equivalent to California's Fresno campus. In the course of his studies, he learned the ways of native and hybrid grapes that grow east of the Rockies. In 1990 Al earned his doctorate following the completion of a dissertation on champagne.

Al admits that making champagne is his first love. Two of his releases at Hermannhof gained the esteemed recognition of judges at the 1990 San Francisco Fair. In this competition, the winery's Brut, a Vidal champagne, and Blanc de Blanc, a blend of Seyval and Villard Blanc grapes, went up against the best of California, taking silver and bronze medals, respectively. Not inclined to boast about this success, Al says, "It's always fun to try a direct comparison to the West Coast."

The winery grows its grapes on forty-two acres surrounding Hermann. The winery enjoys a historical link to the Kropp Brewery of the 1850s, and the vineyards tie their wines to a similarly rich past. Since entering the wine business, Jim and Mary Dierberg have restored the old vintner's cabin about two miles from the winery. Built in 1837 by Julius Ruediger, the homestead overlooks the vineyards where most of Hermannhof's grapes are grown. As a winegrower, Ruediger achieved prominence through his work with George Riefenstahl, Jacob Rommel, and George Husmann, the latter a major contributor to the world history of wine.

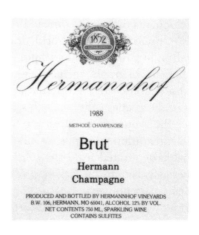

Near Ruediger's cabin Husmann's place faces the Missouri River, flowing imperceptibly in the distant valley below. In one of Husmann's books about winegrowing in America, he described the perfect vineyard site and specifications for the ideal cellar, drawing his recommendations from this farm east of Hermann. The cellar he built there runs north and south the full length of the house, with an opening at the north end. Approximately one-hundred-fifty feet long, twenty-five feet wide, and fifteen feet from the floor to the apex of the arched ceiling, the cellar now contains only the pairs of long, massive timbers where Husmann's barrels once rested.

Hermannhof now maintains Husmann's northeast-facing vineyard, which, in addition to recent plantings of French-American hybrids, also contain what Al Marks describes as "heirloom varieties." Two of Husmann's vine types survive, both *Vitis labrusca*; one he called "Dry Hill Beauty," while the other variety remains an unidentified white grape.

In addition to its achievement in the champagne contest at the San Francisco Fair, Hermannhof displays other national, international, and state honors bestowed on its wines. The 1989 Chambourcin, a dry red wine in the style of France's Rhône valley, won medals at InterVin and from the National Wine Competition of the *Dallas Morning News* in 1990. The off-dry, non-vintage Seyval earned awards at the International Eastern Wine Competition and the Missouri State Fair, while its dry counterpart, the 1989 Seyval, struck gold at the Missouri State Fair in 1990. Other favorites of the judges have included the winery's 1988 Norton and the 1988 Barrel Reserve Vidal. To many Hermannhof fans, the semi-sweet White Lady of Starkenburg remains a reason in itself to visit the winery.

Tours of Hermannhof's extensive cellars illustrate all aspects of the winemaker's art for a nominal fee. Available for purchase at the winery are cheese and sausage, as well as soups and sandwiches. Wine tastes are served free of charge during the winery's hours of operation seven days a week.

Bias Vineyard

Highway 100
Rt. 1, Box 93
Berger MO 63014   (314) 834-5475

Outside of the hamlet of Berger (rhymes with "merger"), Jim and Norma Bias have staked out a hilltop vineyard for the pleasure of their visitors. Not incidentally, they also make wine. When they moved from St. Louis County to Berger in 1978 they found a sorely neglected vineyard, mostly Catawba, on the land they purchased for their winery. Within two years they had replaced ailing *labrusca* vines with cuttings of French-American hybrid varieties, such as Seyval and Vidal.

Located seven miles east of Hermann via Highway 100 and Route B, Bias Vineyards celebrated its tenth anniversary in 1990. Although Jim and Norma still cultivate the original seven-acre vineyard, they have made many improvements beyond restoring the vines. They obviously relish this work and enjoy sharing the fun. Throughout the year Jim and Norma host special events for the friends of the winery. In addition to a schedule of buffet dinners, including an annual chili cook-off, the winery provides a tranquil setting for fall hayrides, self-guided golf-cart tours, and, on special occasions, tram tours of the vineyard.

To accommodate this activity, Bias Vineyards has two miles of trails, an isolated pond and picnic area, and an inviting tasting room complete with a player piano. Jim and Norma expanded the winery in 1990 with a banquet room. From the far wall of the room, a stone fireplace radiates a warm welcome. Jim salvaged the stones of the hearth from one of the nineteenth-century structures on the original farm.

Jim and Norma have no immediate plans to establish more vineyard acreage than they can properly tend themselves. One gets the impression that they tend to the needs of their guests with the same care they apply to their vines, always extending a personal touch. Likewise, they gear their selection of vintage wines to please any palate. Their River View White, a medal winner at the 1990 Missouri State Fair, leads their list of dry white wines, which also includes varietal bottlings

BIAS

VINEYARDS
MISSOURI 1988
RIVER VIEW WHITE
A PREMIUM DRY TABLE WINE
PRODUCED & BOTTLED BY BIAS VINEYARD & WINERY
BERGER, MISSOURI   CONTAINS SULFITES   BONDED WINERY NO. 114

of Vidal and Seyval. Dry red wines, the DeChaunac and Marechal Foch, are also grown, vinted, and bottled at the winery. For those who prefer a touch of sweetness in the wine they drink, Jim and Norma will frequently recommend their Liebeswein, a semi-dry Catawba-Seyval blend that piques one's sense of romance, or their Schöner Frühling, which captures the fragrance and freshness of "beautiful springtime."

A sumptuous feast should always end with dessert. For this part of the meal, a truly unique taste awaits those who give themselves over to Bias Vineyards' mead, the drink of medieval knights and Vikings. As one might expect of fermented honey, the mead is intensely sweet, brightly golden, and a bit thicker than the wines on the Bias menu.

The winery is open for escape from the twentieth-century seven days a week. Even previous visitors to Bias Vineyards will likely find something new at this hilltop hideaway.

Stone Hill II
New Florence

North Outer Road
New Florence MO 63363   (314) 835-2420

Sixteen miles north of Hermann on Highway 19, at the intersection with Interstate 70, Stone Hill II in New Florence offers passing motorists a full brace of Stone Hill wines. More than simply a roadside gift shop for wine enthusiasts, Stone Hill II also functions as a working winery. At this location, Stone Hill produces its award-winning champagne.

Made according to the time-honored prescription of the French, each bottle of Stone Hill's Missouri Champagne goes through secondary fermentation in its own labeled bottle. Called "méthode champenoise," the painstaking process indicates champagne of the finest quality. Bubbles that rise to the surface of a poured glass of Missouri Champagne are typically smaller and livelier than the bubbles of sparkling wine made by the transfer or bulk processes. In the transfer process, the wine indeed ferments in a bottle; however, at the conclusion of this process, individual bottles are emptied into a steel tank for additional processing before returning to the bottle sold to customers. In the bulk, or "charmat" process, all fermentation is carried out in huge steel tanks prior to final bottling. The smoothest sparkling wine bears the phrase "méthode champenoise" or "bottled in *this* bottle" on its label to inform the consumer of its special handling.

The special handling of Missouri Champagne also requires every bottle to be rotated a quarter-turn many times during the secondary fermentation stage. This activity, called "riddling," gathers spent yeast cells in the neck of the downward-angled bottles. Having to turn perhaps thousands of bottles each day, champagne makers of old designed a bottle with a dent in the bottom to facilitate their grip. Once secondary fermentation has finished, the neck of the bottle is frozen and the bottle is uncapped, disgorging a plug of yeasty sediment. Thus freed of yeast cells, the bottle is quickly corked and wired.

In addition to the Brut-style Missouri Champagne, Stone Hill II also makes the semi-sweet Golden Spumante, a fruity accompaniment to picnic-basket fare, and the Spumante Blush, a rosy blend colored by some contact with red grape skins. Youngsters may partake of Stone Hill's sparkling grape juice, a refreshing, no-alcohol blend of Missouri grapes.

In addition to many gift and souvenir items, Stone

Hill II at New Florence also stocks a variety of snacks and a full cold case of cheese and sausage.

Röbller Vineyard

Rt. 1, Box 7
"Old Quarry Road"
New Haven MO 63068   (314) 237-3986

One of the newest wineries on the winemaking map of Missouri, the Röbller Vineyard invites guests to a panoramic view of the rolling hills of the Ozark Plateau from its tasting room near New Haven. Located south of Highway 100 on the gravel "quarry road" east of the New Haven water tower, Röbller Vineyard looks out on a modest start of four and one-half acres of grapevines. Robert and Lois Mueller began planting in 1988, fulfilling a dream they had toyed with for decades. While still living in St. Louis County, this couple had purchased grapes and made wine at home since 1964. When the vineyard site in New Haven came up for sale, they could no longer resist the urge to join the renaissance of Missouri winemaking.

Lois tended the vineyards while Robert built the winery; however, such a division of labor was not exclusive as they, plus members of their family and friends from St. Louis, contributed to the many aspects of bringing the dream into reality. All components of their work-

in-progress point to an April 1991 opening. By that time
the Vidal and Cynthiana fermenting in the wine cellar
will be ready for release; the tasting room will present
the picture of Missouri spring in bloom through long,
plate-glass windows; and Bob and Lois will be watching
the weather forecast with an eye to the protection of their
young vines on the hillsides surrounding their winery.

In addition to the Vidal grapes, the Muellers have
also planted the Steuben, an American red grape hybrid
they intend using in a blush similar to a white Zinfandel.
Other offerings will include a light, semi-dry Cynthiana,
a dry and semi-dry Vidal, and white wine made from
the Melody grape, a Seyval hybrid developed at the New
York State Agricultural Experiment Station in the Finger
Lakes district of New York State. At this time, Robert
and Lois expect to bottle each wine as a varietal. En-
couragement from their St. Louis friends to undertake
such a massive project has been enthusiastic, based on
the Muellers' previous vintages. With such a successful
recipe, they need only time to realize completely the
promptings of a lifetime.

Ozark Highlands

INTERSTATE 44 SLASHES ACROSS MISSOURI FROM St. Louis to Joplin in a hurry. Formerly the legendary Route 66, it is the quickest way to drive to Oklahoma City, Gallup, Flagstaff, San Bernardino, and the West Coast. As an interstate highway, this westward artery has evolved into merely a means to an end; the romance of the route passes in a blur.

Occasionally, I-44 brushes ramshackle motels of a bygone age of American motor travel. St. Clair, about a half-hour southwest of St. Louis, distinguishes itself with hot- and cold-water towers to amuse the fancy of passing tourists. Billboards invite travelers to visit Meramec Caverns, Jesse James's alleged hideout, and Onondaga Cave.

Other than to stretch, use a restroom, change drivers, and fill up on burgers, travelers have little inclination to stop before they have put in a long shift behind the wheel. They might not realize they are in the Ozark Highlands viticultural area as they enter Phelps and Crawford counties; they might not notice the vineyards along the road near St. James. They might never know that just beyond view from the interstate lies some of the most beautiful countryside that Missouri has to offer.

Because of these attributes of the land, bicycle enthusiasts regard St. James as a destination in itself. Twice a year, in the spring and fall, the St. Louis Bicycle Club sponsors tours that originate at the tourist information center of St. James, located at the intersection of Highway 68 and Interstate 44.

Well-maintained, two-lane asphalt trails link St. James with the outlying communities of Flag Springs, Rosati, Cuba, Steelville, and Rolla. With dense hardwood forests and a narrow gravel shoulder on either side, these country roads test the cornering ability of any car. For cyclists, the gently rolling hills provide a moderate challenge.

The topographical features that make the Ozark

OZARK HIGHLANDS

♦ winery

Highlands an attractive course for cyclists also aid the grape farmers in the area. In general, the plateau around St. James, known as Big Prairie, differs from the hill country of the Ozarks. Unlike many vineyard areas on sloping river valleys, this upland ''prairie'' is lightly striated with sinewy ridges. An elevation generally higher than much of the surrounding landscape sheds the cold air in early fall and late spring to valleys over the edge of the prairie. As much to the benefit of grape growers as the lay of the land, Big Prairie encompasses a rich layer of clay loam, instead of the cherty limestone soil that characterizes much of the Ozark Plateau.

Even to this day, wild grapevines thrive in the soil of the prairie just as Gottfried Duden had described them in the forests of Warren County. Huge, muscular canes wind up the trunks of elms, reaching for the sun in the leafy boughs high above the ground.

The cultivation of grapes in Phelps County predates

the Italian settlement at Rosati. When the Atlantic & Pacific Railroad, forerunner of the St. Louis-San Francisco Railroad, brought trains from St. Louis to Rolla, it immediately promoted the area for agriculture. After the Civil War, the railroad brought carloads of Swedes and Danes to Rolla directly from their port of entry on the East Coast. Germans in Rolla reported a twenty-five acre start at viniculture in 1870. The Soest & Bros. vineyard there grew Catawba, Concord, and Norton.

Handbills in the 1870s attracted a few French families to take up residence in Dillon, a now-indistinct community midway between Rolla and St. James. Some thirty years later these French welcomed the Italians to Rosati with grape vine cuttings for their family gardens. At the outset of Prohibition in 1919, the grape growers in Rosati closed their ranks by forming the Knobview Fruit Growers Association. They expanded the vineyards during the fourteen-year ''noble experiment,'' shipping Concord grapes to Welch's Grape Juice company in Springdale, Arkansas.

Located within the boundaries of the Ozark Mountain Viticultural Area—which takes in virtually all of the state south of the Missouri River, as well as parts of Oklahoma and Arkansas—the Ozark Highlands viticultural area is bordered by the rivers and ridges that skirt the prairie. The tourist information center of St. James serves as a convenient starting point for a wine tour. The center's staff can provide travelers with extensive information about accommodations and other attractions in the area.

St. James Winery

540 Sidney Street
St. James MO 65559   (314) 265-7912

Less than a mile east of the tourist information center, on Route B, which at that point runs along the north side of Interstate 44, the St. James Winery exhibits a bunch of stained-glass blue grapes the size of a pickup truck. Owned and operated by James and Patricia

Hofherr since 1970, the winery now employs the skills of two Hofherr sons, John and Andrew. Trained in enology and viticulture at the California State University at Fresno, John has brought a decidedly West Coast flavor to the winery and the wines. Knowing full well that his success as winemaker depends on the quality of the grapes he receives, John applauds the work of Andrew, who manages the family vineyards and cares for the monstrous machine that gently harvests the grapes. Based on the commitment to viticulture made by their parents in 1970, the skills of John and Andrew complement each other.

Two styles of wine are made at the St. James Winery: the premium wines of the Friendship School label and the traditional favorites, including sparkling Concord and Niagara grape juices and apple cider. About two miles distant, the winery grows its own grapes on seventy acres across from the former Friendship School, once attended by children of the early Rosati settlers, now used as a community center. In 1989 the winery won medals at the Missouri State Fair for its Schoolhouse White, a semi-dry blend of mainly native Delaware grapes, its Velvet Red wine, and its Sparkling Niagara grape juice. It also won a silver medal at the International Eastern Wine Competition for its 1988 Seyval and a bronze medal at the Atlanta International Wine Show for its 1988 barrel-aged Seyval.

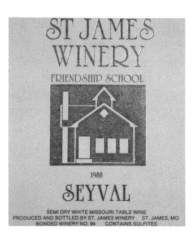

Further indication of Hofherr success came in 1990 with a first place ribbon at the Indiana State Fair for its Blush, a semi-sweet rosé blend of Seyval and Cayuga grapes. This award is a matter of some pride to Pat Hofherr because she and Jim originally hail from there. In addition, the Hofherrs took home ''Best of Show'' honors at the Missouri State Fair with their off-dry 1989 Seyval Blanc. Other medals at this year's Missouri State Fair recognized the winery's Concord and Sparkling Niagara grape juices, the 1988 Chancellor, a dry, red wine aged in oak barrels, and the off-dry 1989 Vignoles and Cayuga White wines.

St. James Winery also continues an Ozarks tradition in fermented juices made from blackberries, strawberries, loganberries, and raspberries. The gift shop makes available a large selection of hard-to-find winemaking supplies, as well as wine glassware, cheese, and other wine-related gifts and souvenirs. The winery conducts free tours of its modern facility—a little bit of California in the heartland—seven days a week.

Ferrigno Winery

Highway B
Rt. 2, P.O. Box 227
St. James MO 65559   (314) 265-7742

Four and one-half miles farther on Route B brings the wine traveler to the Ferrigno Winery on the west side of the two-lane blacktop. Straight past a winery direction sign at the Route U intersection, the curving country road passes Flag Springs and a kennel before rounding a bend to the wide-open vineyard prairie. An old dairy barn clad in richly weathered wood sits by the roadside, a ''Welcome'' sign resting next to the open door.

Dick and Susan Ferrigno abandoned their Central West End lifestyle in St. Louis when they opened the winery in 1981. Before they moved, they had considered Oregon and Europe as possible locations for their new adventure. Of primary importance to them was the desire to make a regionally distinctive wine, much like the small chateau wineries of the French countryside. Dick still insists on "regional integrity" as he displays the fruits of this dream in wines made entirely from Missouri grapes.

Like other winemakers in the St. James area, the couple was attracted to the viticultural history of the region. Their vineyard, currently sixteen acres that immediately surround the winery, has roots to the Prohibition-era days of Welch's Grape Juice Cooperative. These days, however, the rows of wire support vines of French hybrid grapes: Vidal, Chambourcin, Chelois, and Seyval; as well as native *labrusca* varieties, such as Missouri Riesling, Niagara, and Concord.

Produced and Bottled by Ferrigno Vineyards and Winery
St. James, Missouri   BW-MO-119   Contains Sulfites

From the upper deck of the winery's wine garden, the vineyards stretch to the west across well-drained rolling fields. Here visitors can relax in cool comfort as they enjoy a Missouri picnic. Throughout the summer, the wine garden pavilion is the scene of the Ferrigno Winery's dinner-concert series. In 1990 six concerts in the series featured jazz, classical, folk, Cajun, R&B, and rock performers. On each of these nights, hosts Susan and Dick created a lavish theme dinner to complement the music.

The success of the dinner and concert series is reflected in requests that Susan and Dick receive to cater private parties at the winery. These have included wedding rehearsal dinners and receptions and even an encampment of medievalists. The winery also offers bed-and-breakfast accommodations, including a romantic, secluded loft above the winery.

As former urbanites, the Ferrignos have carefully designed a relaxing retreat. Next to the winery, a split-level home, complete with kitchen, offers overnighters the Seyval and Vidal rooms. Though the rooms share the bathroom and the kitchen, each has its own parlor. The Vidal room also features a fireplace and sofa bed in its living room. For many people who live in a city, it is hard to imagine—much less remember—a night without the television, the radio, the telephone; it is hard even to fantasize about spending a cool evening on a screened porch in conversation; it is difficult to count one second of silence between the passing of traffic on the street. At the Ferrigno Winery, the solace of a cool country evening soothes the urgency, alarm, and congestion of modern life.

Dick Ferrigno philosophizes that some wines are crafted to win awards, others are made to be enjoyed at the table. That's not to say that his wines have not won their share of honors. For example, the winery took home medals in the 1985 Missouri State Fair for two red wines: the semi-dry Vino Di Famiglia, a fine accompaniment to hearty Italian fare and spicy barbecue; and the dry, Bordeaux-style 1982 Chelois. The winery also offers white wine fans a dry, tart Seyval Blanc, a semi-dry Vidal Blanc, full of luscious, buttery-smooth flavor, and the zesty Primavera semi-dry blend that hints of the spice rack. A dry, oak-aged Chambourcin rounds out the selection of red dinner wines as an excellent accompaniment to hearty soups, beef, and game.

In all, the Ferrigno Winery offers a dozen wines ranging from dry to sweet dessert wine blends, including a "blush" or *blanc de noir* wine made from de Chaunac grapes and a semi-sweet rosé, called Garden Blush, from Concord grapes. Samples of all the wines are available for tasting in the hospitality room above the winery. Missouri cheeses, sausages, and home-grown fruit in season are also available for a picnic in the wine garden. Souvenirs and collectibles are offered in the gift shop.

Heinrichshaus Vineyards & Winery

Rt. 2, Box 2102
St. James MO 65559   (314) 265-5000

For those in search of dusty country roads, there is a scenic route of one-lane bypaths from Ferrigno Winery to Heinrichshaus Vineyards & Winery. Others who feel more comfortable on pavement can backtrack on Route B to the intersection of Route U. There, a sign points the traveler eastward to Heinrichshaus.

Tucked away in a shady copse of elms, Heinrichshaus enables visitors to leave the worries of the world behind. The proprieter, Heinrich Grohe, takes pride in having built the winery—except for the concrete slab—himself. He speaks of it lovingly, as the work of a lifetime.

Originally from the Black Forest region of the Rhine Valley, Heinrich brought winemaking skills with him to this country in the 1950s. Although a few years passed before he could satisfy his desire to make wine as his forebears had done, he eventually chose the Ozark Highlands and opened his winery in 1979. In the *Fachwerk*-style of timber and stucco, the winery embodies the man's background; here, a visitor may be transported to a *Weinstube* in the foothills of the Swiss Alps.

The high standard of craft Heinrich applied to the construction of the winery applies to his winemaker's art as well. ''Quality comes first,'' he proclaims, even though he prefers the title of winegrower to that of winemaker. His distinction is in letting the natural process of fermentation take place with as little human intrusion as possible. In nature, wild yeast collects in the chalky dullness on the skin of the grapes called ''bloom.'' Once the yeast has performed its function in converting the sugar in the grape into alcohol and carbon dioxide, the winemaker steps in to decide the fate of the juice, whether it should age in wooden casks and for how long, whether its best features would shine through in a blend or deserve a varietal bottling. Heinrich treats each wine as unique, each with an individual character that determines its future.

More than the other winegrowers of the Ozark

Highlands, Heinrich confidently promotes Cynthiana as the grape of Missouri winemaking's former glory and rebirth. Although the vineyards contain other varieties that make equally palatable wine, such as French hybrids Seyval, Vidal, Baco Noir, and Chambourcin, and the native Catawba, Heinrich cites Cynthiana's resistance to disease, hardiness at unexpected frost, and output. Like the winegrower himself, the grapes seem to thrive in the Ozark Highlands.

vintage 1985

HEINRICHSHAUS

Missouri
BACO NOIR

*a dry, spicy red table wine
made entirely from the Baco Noir grape
grown, vinted and cellared in Missouri*

Produced and bottled by HEINRICHSHAUS VINEYARDS AND WINERY
St. James, Missouri — Missouri Bonded Winery 107

CONTAINS SULFITES

In recent years Heinrich and Lois Grohe have been joined in their craft by their daughter and son-in-law. Along with their youthful self-assurance and energy, Peggy and Jean-Phillip Bolle apply their backgrounds in viticulture to continue the Grohe tradition: ''Quality comes first.'' Their commitment has been recognized in part at the Missouri State Fair. In 1989, Heinrichshaus won medals for its 1988 Vidal Blanc and its 1988 Cynthiana. The following year brought awards to the 1989 Missouri Vidal Blanc, the dry Prairie Gold white wine blend, the Prairie Rosé, and the white Weingarten semi-dry blend.

On a visit to Heinrichshaus, wine lovers will find handcrafted wines available nowhere else. This limited point of distribution allows Heinrich and his family to offer wine at a price reasonable enough for everyday dining. The winery also carries a selection of other Missouri hand-crafted items.

Mt. Pleasant Winery
Abbey Vineyard

Rt. 3, Box 199
I-44 at Route UU
Cuba MO 65453   (314) 885-2168

Visitors to Mt. Pleasant's Abbey Vineyard, two miles east of Cuba, Missouri, at the Route UU exit from I-44, comprise a surprising mix of people. Many express their disbelief at finding a winery in Missouri; many of the same will soon delight in the Mt. Pleasant wines inside.

In another industry, perhaps walnut bowls or cowboy boots, Mt. Pleasant's Abbey Vineyard might be dismissed as merely a factory outlet. Yet, at this location, an important part of the winemaker's craft happens in the former gas station repair bay. Without fanfare, Mt. Pleasant's famed Port quietly ages in a pyramid of oak barrels.

In addition to a complete selection of Mt. Pleasant wines, the Abbey Vineyard offers the curious passerby an enjoyable detour from the doldrums of interstate travel. A few visitors to the Abbey Vineyard are well acquainted with the world of wine; mostly, however, people

pull off the interstate looking for a novelty, a place to relieve highway hypnosis, or space for children to release energy. Not infrequently, car problems bring travelers to the tasting room to summon road service. The Abbey Vineyard provides these amenities and more.

The vineyard's staff customizes their tours for visitors, concisely covering viticulture in Missouri, the differences between *vinifera* and native species, and the process by which grape juice turns into wine. Displays make the tour as thorough as any given in a "real" working winery. There are an antiquated crusher, a small wine press, a wooden fermentation vat, barrels of aging wine, and, of course, the end result, fine wine. More important than the old machinery are the vineyards surrounding the converted interstate restaurant. At this location Mt. Pleasant grows Pearl of Oman grapes on seven acres. These grapes go into making Pearl of Oman champagne at the winery in Augusta.

Of particular interest to many people who sidle up to the tasting bar are the Abbey Vineyard fruit wines unavailable elsewhere. A sip of these light, sweet blends of white wine and berry juice quenches the thirst on a hot August day in Missouri. While Raspberry Smash, Strawberry Smash, and Blackberry Smash are the most consistently available wines in this style, the winery will occasionally bottle Peach Smash. Not technically a wine (since no grapes are involved), Peach Smash combines fermented honey—that is, mead—and peach juice to create a beverage of truly sublime sweetness.

For many travelers through the State of Missouri, Mt. Pleasant's Abbey Vineyard serves a useful purpose in displaying some of the fine wines that have contributed to the renaissance of winemaking here. In addition to a full menu of the winery's offerings, including Concord grape juice and apple cider, the Abbey Vineyard also features many kinds of Missouri cheeses and sausages, as well as gifts and mementos.

Peaceful Bend Vineyard

Rt. 2, Box 544
Route T
Steelville MO 65565   (314) 775-2578

Peaceful Bend Vineyard has enjoyed quiet success as a winery since 1972. Perched above a serpentine stretch of the Meramec River, the winery is located two miles west of Steelville on Route 8 and two miles north on Route T. This part of the Ozark Highlands viticultural area has been long noted for its pristine streams—the upper Meramec, and its tributaries, the Courtois (pronounced ''coat-away'') and the Huzzah.

Since its opening, Peaceful Bend Vineyard has provisioned many float trips with wine. Thus, it takes names of the local streams for its selections. Nearly year around, canoeists haul their craft through narrow access roads to float the river.

Now that Missourians have become more knowledgeable about wine, the significant role of Peaceful Bend in the renaissance of Missouri winemaking has come to light. Dr. A. N. Arneson started planting French hybrid grapes on the slopes around the future winery in 1965. A physican at Barnes Hospital in St. Louis, Arneson found a few occasions where his interest in winemaking enhanced his medical career.

Through a colleague he met at a conference, Arneson became acquainted with Philip Wagner, whose knowledge about French-American hybrid grape varieties infused the moribund winemaking regions east of the Rockies with new life. In 1956 Arneson brought French hybrids to Missouri from the Wagner's Maryland nurseries. Appropriately, many winemakers in the Ozark Highlands give credit to Arneson, a gynecologist, for ''mid-wifing'' the cultivation of wine grapes in Missouri between the repeal of Prohibition and the reawakening of the vineyards in the mid-1960s. His vast store of information about the history of viticulture in this state is now being acknowledged.

Also indicative of Arneson's link with the history of winemaking in Missouri is equipment he acquired from

St. Stanislaus Seminary in St. Louis County when the Jesuits closed their winery in 1960. The crusher used for many years there now sits atop the Peaceful Bend winery, still in operation. Arneson also purchased a hundred-gallon oak barrel, which rests as a museum piece in a corner of the winery.

Now retired from medical practice, Arneson still blends wine that goes into his uniquely named vintages. He attributes the continued success of Peaceful Bend Vineyard to the skill and care of his vineyard manager, Bob DeWitt. DeWitt joined the winery in 1986 at a time when, as Arneson admits, the vineyard showed signs of neglect. Schooled in horticulture and forestry, Bob is most comfortable among the vines. They have responded to his care like orphaned children in need of love. After four years of Bob's care, the harvest in 1990 realized substantial gains in quality and quantity.

WITTENBURG CREEK

Crawford County
White Table Wine

PRODUCED AND BOTTLED BY
PEACEFUL BEND VINEYARD
STEELVILLE, MISSOURI

Even though a number of years have passed since Peaceful Bend Vineyard entered at the Missouri State Fair, the winery has maintained its commitment to making blended wines of quality from French-American hybrid grapes. The available styles in red and white wines range from dry to sweet. The winery offers free tastes of its wines and the pleasure of viewing some of most scenic woodlands in Missouri.

Reis Winery

Rt. 4, Box 133
Route CC
Licking MO 65542　　　　　　　　(314) 674-3763

Located thirty-some miles south of Rolla on Highway 63, Reis Winery welcomes visitors with its own 2,600-foot grass airstrip. Dr. Val and Joy Reis planted the vineyard on Route CC near Maples, Missouri, in 1972 to make dry wine, then a rarity in Missouri. Over the next six years, they established an eight-acre vineyard of French hybrid grapes, also a rarity in Missouri at that time. Driven by a preference for dry wines on their own dinner table, they procured their initial nursery stock from Philip Wagner's Boordy Vineyard in Maryland. Soon after opening the winery in 1978, Reis Winery had no fewer than thirty varieties in production.

Although the winery's proximity to Montauk State Park frequently lures trout fishers, hikers, and campers to the Reis Winery tasting room, Val and Joy admit they do not attract many casual travelers from I-44. Because Maples is somewhat removed from the other wineries of the Ozark Highlands viticultural area, the Reis family decided to open a branch tasting room at the Lake of the Ozarks (see Wine Tour Six, Mid-Missouri). This latest endeavor often requires Joy, the tasting room hostess, to divide her time between the two places. Nonetheless, whenever Jim and Pam Reis can spare her from the Lake Ozark Winery, Joy hangs out her ''Open'' sign at the original location.

Most of the visitors to Reis Winery in Maples, whether they arrive by car or by plane, come with a purpose: to restock their cellars with Reis wines. Following the style of the French, Val and Joy Reis combine wine in making a *cuvée*, or blend, for several selections, such as their Burgundy and their Rhine wines. Among the current list of twelve wines made at the winery, four grape types are vinted as varietal wines. One expects to find Seyval and Vidal varietals at a Missouri winery. Yet Val and Joy add a personal touch to these wines with a trace of Chardonnay in the Seyval and a hint of Johannisberg

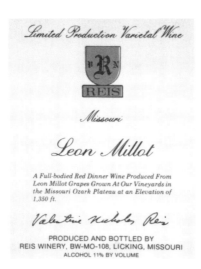

Riesling in their Vidal. Like all the grapes that go into Reis wines, both *viníferas* are also grown in the Ozark Highland viticultural area. In addition, the Reises bottle a dry, red Leon Millot and a Villard Blanc as much-sought-after varietals. Since 1978 Reis Winery has won a number of awards for their wines in state fair competitions in Missouri and Indiana.

While Joy believes dry wines generally accompany meals better than most sweet wines, she and her husband decided to add sweet wines to their menu to satisfy the sweet tooth of many of their visitors. In addition to Pink Catawba and a deeply colored and aromatic Concord, the family makes a pure cherry wine from the fruit of their own trees. When they have time and materials on hand, they make two other natural fruit wines from strawberry juice and blackberry juice. Like the cherry wine, these contain only the fermented juice of fresh fruit.

At an elevation of 1,350 feet, Reis Winery claims to be one of the highest in the state. While the topography of the Ozark Plateau, an upland prairie, conceals this height in rolling hills and winding inclines, many friends of the winery enjoy the unhurried pace of driving the back roads of the viticultural area. Travelers who take the time to discover Reis Winery will find a congenial welcome, a selection of cheeses and snack items to purchase, and country wines made in an Old World style.

Tour Four

Ozark Mountains

THE SOUTHWEST CORNER OF MISSOURI BECAME a part of the world's winemaking map in the late 1800s when the French government bestowed its Legion of Honor medal on a resident of Neosho. Hermann Jaeger (pronounced "Yaeger"), a Swiss immigrant who had come to Missouri at the conclusion of the Civil War, landed in Newton County, seemingly by the whim of the railroad. In Europe he had worked in dry goods and, briefly, at a winery. In Missouri he nurtured a keen interest in viticulture, making 150 gallons of Concord wine in 1869, which he touted as "the first wine made this side of Springfield." On Oliver's Prairie, about three and a half miles south of the prosperous lead mining town of Granby, Jaeger established his "New Swiss Vineyard," where he carried out extensive experiments in cross pollenating native American grape species, such as *aestavalis, riparia, rupestris,* and *lincecumii.*

In the 1870s Jaeger shipped tons of his pest-resistant rootstock, chiefly *riparia* and *rupestris,* to France, where infestation by the *Phylloxera* louse had nearly wiped out the classic wine-grape vineyards. In a last-ditch effort to save their vines, French *vignerons* grafted their varieties onto Jaeger's rootstock. The American rootstock resisted the deadly attack of the *Phylloxera*; what's more, the new roots did not seem to affect the subtle taste and aroma characteristics of the *vinifera* wine grapes they supported.

Vineyards around the world turned back the onslaught of *Phylloxera* in the same way, many using later generations of the stock Jaeger shipped to France. The French government recognized Jaeger's contribution, along with that of his friend T. V. Munson, in 1888. In 1895, discouraged by the local opposition to winemaking, Jaeger turned his back on his vineyard and walked way, leaving no further trace.

John Jaeger continued his brother's New Swiss Vineyard, despite growing resentment from the temperance militants among his neighbors. At one point a Newton County court indicted John Jaeger with charges of allowing a visitor to consume wine on the premises. For years the self-righteous moral guardians of Newton County had looked with disdain on the Jaegers' vineyard and winery. On Sundays, miners and their families from nearby Granby were known to while away the afternoon in the company of the devil at the *Weingarten*. It was rumored that some even danced. Through an appeal to the Missouri Supreme Court, the indictment was overturned. Nonetheless, its damage had been done. John Jaeger committed suicide in 1906.

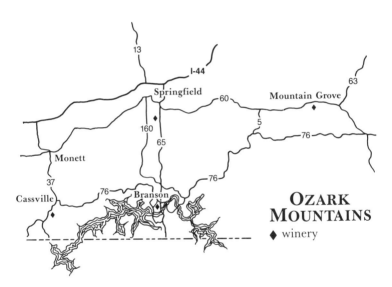

O'Vallon Winery

Rt. 1, Box 77B
Highway 37
Washburn MO 65772   (417) 826-5830

Today, Hermann Jaeger's dedication is carried on by Dr.
Frank England, the winemaker of O'Vallon Winery. Feeling a kinship of purpose with the Swiss immigrant,
England has attempted to perpetuate Jaeger's memory
in the wine he makes and in the vineyard he has planted.

Located about sixty-five miles southeast of Joplin on
Highway 37, O'Vallon appears as an oasis in the Ozarks
for the wine lover. Without too much prodding, Frank
will happily explain the rich winemaking tradition of his
part of the state and the contribution of Hermann Jaeger
that saved the vineyards of the world.

One of England's goals has been to collect and
cultivate any remaining descendants of Jaeger's New
Swiss Vineyard experiments. Most of the grape varieties
developed by Jaeger have vanished, like their founder,
without a trace. Others, such as those he sent to Europe
in the 1870s, live on as the roots of plants there. Still
others appear in the genealogy of the hybrid grapes
developed in France and now planted throughout states
east of the Rockies.

Established in 1987, O'Vallon takes its name from a
contraction of "Haut Vallon," meaning "high valley"
in French. In its first year of operation, the winery took
four medals in Missouri State Fair competition, a gold
each for the semi-dry Vidal and the French-oak-aged
Vignoles. A modest, down-to-earth man, Frank attributes much of his success to the grapes he uses. "If
you have the right chemistry in the grape, good wine
will almost make itself," he says, using Vignoles as an
apt illustration. With near-perfect balance of acid and
sugar, Vignoles has earned Frank's praise as "Missouri's
noble grape."

Like Hermann Jaeger, Frank England has also
achieved success in making wine from *Vitis aestavalis*
grapes, that is, Nortons. He does not discourage comparison of this wine with California's spicy Zinfandel;

he actually seems surprised to find the two deep red, robust wines mentioned in the same breath. Similarly, his Chambourcin begs for comparison to a berry-rich Cabernet Sauvignon, and his 1989 Vidal would receive as many raves as a well-made Chardonnay if they showed up at the same table. The judges at the 1990 Missouri State Fair chose two O'Vallon blends, the dry white Melange à Trois and the Evening Shade, a semi-dry white, as among the best in the state.

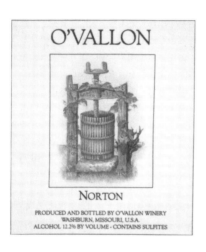

Rather than flaunt these and other awards, however, Frank prefers to show a contemporary photograph of the cast-iron yoke of Hermann Jaeger's wine press, from which O'Vallon's label takes its design. He is even more pleased to see guests at his *Weingarten* restaurant enjoy the wine they have selected to accompany their dinner. On summer weekend evenings, the *Weingarten* features a bill of fare colored by many German specialties, such as rouladen, Jaeger schnitzel (not named for Hermann), and sauerbraten. For such foods, Frank recommends the Riesling-like 1989 Vignoles or, his personal favorite, the Vidal. Just as often, his guests will ask for one of his medal-winning whites.

Stone Hill Wine
& Juice Company

HCR #5, Box 1825
Highway 165
Branson MO 65616   (417) 334-1897

Branson combines the bright lights of Las Vegas, the religious fervor of Jerusalem, and the fun of Disneyland in a resort area that has moved into the top-ten list of vacation destinations in the United States. Long noted as the setting for Harold Bell Wright's novel *The Shepherd of the Hills*, this mountainous region features an extensive display of Ozark and pioneer crafts at Silver Dollar City. It has also attracted renowned country singers— Mel Tillis, Christy Lane, Roy Clark, Box Car Willie, and others—from Nashville to its theaters. As a result of these developments, Branson has evolved from a secluded fishin' hole stocked with lunker trout to a year-round resort community of family-style country attractions.

As current vice-president of the Branson Chamber of Commerce, Thomas Held believes the community is just now beginning to realize its potential. In 1990 more than four million visitors came to Branson. Like other entrepreneurs in Branson, Held needs no additional data to dream of an exciting future for the Ozarks. Of that 1990 crowd, about a quarter-of-a-million people toured his Stone Hill Wine and Juice Company.

At "Stone Hill III," visitors follow guides through a brief, well-illustrated tour of the winemaking process. A short video sets the stage with an overview of the winemaking heritage of Missouri. After passing a display of oak cooperage, the guide gives special emphasis to the procedure by which Stone Hill III bottles its Spumantes, or sparkling wines, the leading seller at this location. Other parts of the process are explained on the path that leads to the tasting counter. Once positioned around the counter, the visitors receive further enlightenment in the form of samples poured by their guide. These tastes take the visiting palates through the repertoire of Stone Hill wines from dry to sweet.

STONE HILL
SPARKLING GRAPE JUICE
NATURALLY SWEET UNFERMENTED
PRODUCED AND BOTTLED BY STONE HILL WINERY
IN BRANSON, MISSOURI

Bottling the Spumante is the only aspect of the winemaking process carried out at the Branson branch of Hermann's Stone Hill Wine Company (see Wine Tour Two—Hermann). Opened in 1986, Stone Hill Wine & Juice Company began as the parent firm's off-site research laboratory. In the relative isolation of the Ozark Mountains, Held, a graduate of the University of Arkansas food science curriculum, experimented with the techniques he learned at the university winery. Under such favorable circumstances, Held made trial batches of blends and varietals that Stone Hill considered for future release. Eventually, however, the rapidly rising number of visitors to the winery diverted his attention from lab work to the tasting room and gift shop.

Today Held contemplates the many ways visitors can carry the Stone Hill experience with them. He not infrequently finds a young couple has been directed to the winery by grandparents who came earlier, perhaps on a bus tour. At the tasting counter of Stone Hill III, samples transform the mystery of a bottle with a hard-to-pronounce name into a beverage Missourians can serve with pride.

Ozark Vineyard Winery

Highway 65
Chestnutridge MO 65630   (417) 587-3555

A few miles north of Branson on Highway 65, Ozark

Vineyard Winery at Chestnutridge perches high above the steeply sloping "hollers" like a Rhine valley fortress. The valley is as deep and rugged as the scenery pictured in Hollywood's version of *The Shepherd of the Hills*. Though the valley elevates the rather simple structure to a *Schloss* comparison, the one word, WINERY, in bold green block letters unequivocally states its purpose.

Hershel Gray claimed this high ground for Ozark Vineyard Winery in 1976. Years before he decided to open a winery on the northern approach to Branson, he grew grapes for export to New York and Ohio. Because of a poor market, he began pressing his crop of native and hybrid grapes for his own distinctive blends. Recently, the rising costs associated with growing grapes led him to buy his raw materials from other Missouri vineyards, a business decision that allows him to focus on making wine and tending the tasting counter.

Catawba is the only grape that Hershel bottles as a varietal; Ozark Vineyard offers two types, a white and a pink. Other releases, as their proprietary names suggest, are Hershel's own blends, ranging from the sweet Ozark Red to the semi-dry Bonny Brook blush to the dry White River White. In making these wines, Hershel avoids the use of oak barrel aging. Other winemakers throughout the world believe that oak works a magical transformation on fine wine, adding a subtle complexity. As a modern winemaker, Hershel views the use of oak barrels as so much hocus pocus. In fact, he thinks winemakers should be cautious in employing oak cooperage, asking if the risk is worth the perpetuating the tradition.

In addition to samples of Ozark Vineyard wines, visitors will find a selection of cheese, sausage, and bread at the winery, as well as grape juice in season. Although the winery is open during regular business hours on Friday and Saturday only, Herschel admits that most days find him there.

State Fruit Experiment Station
Southwest Missouri State University

Rt. 3, Box 63
Mountain Grove MO 65711   (417) 926-4105

Although not a commercial winery in purpose, the State Fruit Experiment Station grows many acres of grapes and processes its annual yield to explore the complicated chemistry of wine. While viticulture and winemaking are not the only research pursuits at the station, they have received significant funding from the state since the Missouri General Assembly instituted a four-cent-per-gallon tax on wine in 1984. This money has allowed the state to support full-time positions in enology and viticulture, as well as ancillary staff, facilities, and programs.

According to Dr. James Moore, director of the station, the degree of effort aimed toward grape and wine research, like the tax itself, is a direct result of the self-promotional activities of Missouri grape growers, who, through their trade associations, have succeeded in influencing decision-makers in Jefferson City to dismantle the vestiges of Prohibition remaining in state laws. In addition, the grape growers take full advantage of the resources of the State Fruit Experiment Station, which became a part of Southwest Missouri State University in the mid 1970s. The expertise of researchers at the station is the key to finding the grape varieties that will produce Missouri's own versions of Chardonnay and Cabernet wines.

The top goal on Dr. Moore's list of priorities is to find the varieties most suited to Missouri growing conditions. Second, research at the station aims to find ways of reducing one of the grape growers' biggests costs, the chemicals used to ward off pests and diseases. The carefully laid-out rows also test the effects of vineyard management techniques on grape crops. Despite the coordinated focus of research, none of the thirteen grape varieties released by the station has become Missouri's ''wonder grape'' for winemaking.

That's not for lack of trying. The station has been engaged in viticulture since its founding in 1899. From the outset it planted European types, primarily for breeding stock. Scores of new varieties from all over the world arrive at the station to undergo the first critical test of life in Missouri: winter hardiness. Most fail. In addition to the legions of pests common to winemaking regions throughout the eastern United States, Moore cites the fluctuations of temperature and the high humidity of Missouri as other threats to new varieties that arrive at the station.

Such adversity has not daunted the expectations of Missouri winemakers, either those of the nineteenth century or those of the present. Viticulture research of today, meanwhile, makes regular advances in technology and science. To speed this information from the universities to the winegrowers is a chief responsibility of Dr. Murli Dharmadhikari, Missouri's state enology advisor since 1986. According to Dharmadhikari, the role of advisors at the station is to consult with winegrowers through on-site visits, to conduct seminars on recent research, and to analyze grapes and wine under state-of-the-art laboratory conditions. Missouri's new viticulture adviser at the station is Dr. Charles Edson, a recent graduate of Michigan State University.

The State Fruit Experiment Station deserves a prominent place on the winemaking map of Missouri. In addition, a wide range of interests brings many amateur and professional growers to the station throughout the year. Some might be raising strawberries for a living;

some might be tending a peach orchard in the Bootheel; others might have a finicky trick apple tree in the backyard. In Mountain Grove, the experts of the State Fruit Experiment Station freely share their knowledge about the challenges and advantages of growing fruit in Missouri.

Mountain Grove itself also attracts visitors from throughout the Midwest. Noted as the ''gateway to the old mill trail,'' the city serves as the starting point for a tour of six water-operated mills of the nineteenth century. The power generated by these mills ground grain and sawed lumber for the first settlers in the area. Less than two hundred miles from both St. Louis and Kansas City, the region draws sport fishing enthusiasts. In addition to ten public access points to rivers in the area, Mountain Grove paves the way to outdoor recreation at Bull Shoals Lake and Norfork Lake.

WESTERN MISSOURI

MIDWAY BETWEEN ST. LOUIS AND KANSAS CITY the American West begins. Where I-70 crosses the Missouri River at Rocheport, the craggy hills of the Ozark Plateau become undulating swells of grassland. In the late 1820s steamboats ferried pioneers and entrepreneurs up the Missouri River as far as the mouth of the Kaw, the tributary known later as the Kansas River. Here, the Missouri's sharp turn north diverted pioneers to overland routes. Near this junction of rivers and trails, merchants, traders, and missionaries took advantage of the location as the nation's threshold to the frontier.

As the federal government relinquished its control of the fur trade, private companies moved to Missouri's western border to engage in this lucrative business. Trade with Indians comprised most of the early commerce. A link was also formed with the Mexican settlement at Santa Fe, where premium prices were paid for manufactured goods. With the end of the Mexican War and the discovery of gold in California in 1848, traffic through Missouri increased dramatically. At the same time, the great number of Americans migrating to the Pacific Northwest made Manifest Destiny a reality.

Kansas City

In the two decades before the Civil War, supplying the throng of travelers brought prosperity to several communities on the edge of the frontier. The "City of Kansas" (originally known as Westport Landing) competed fiercely with Independence, Leavenworth, and St. Joseph for the western trade.

As bright as the antebellum period was, the Civil War years were dark. The prospects for Kansas City's future dimmed. Anti-slavery Jayhawkers from Kansas clashed with pro-Southern guerillas along the border between

the two states. As the danger increased in Kansas City, businesses evacuated the area.

The arrival of the Missouri Pacific Railroad in 1865 resuscitated Kansas City and secured its lead as a boomtown. As the railhead to markets in the East, it later attracted cattle from Texas and grain shipments from Kansas.

Even today the appearance and character of western Missouri reflect a frontier spirit that differs from the staid, urbane cities to the east. The city limits reach past the outerbelt highway I-435, where glimpses of prairie bring back the days of the covered wagon. In the distance, skyscrapers of glass, steel, and concrete bunch together as an outcropping of rock.

Prior to Prohibition, viniculture existed in many of the cities of the area. Across the Missouri River from Weston, John Burr and Dr. Joseph Stayman separately produced new grape hybrids in their Leavenworth vineyards as early as 1860. Stayman earned everlasting fame for the apple variety named after him.

In the Kansas City of 1870, one hundred acres of wine grapes were cultivated, according to the *Report of the Commissioner of Agriculture.* As a result of Prohibition, interest in growing wine grapes lay dormant much of the twentieth century. It was not until the 1970s that the renaissance of Missouri winemaking aroused a few adventurous souls to revive this part of Missouri's heritage.

Spring Creek Winery

111 South Eighth Street
Blue Springs MO 64015   (816) 229-7959

At Spring Creek Winery, Kelly McDonald shares with her guests a belief she has held for her entire adult life: that Missouri produces fine wines. When she lived in Labadie, a small town across the river from Augusta, she learned to appreciate wine by sampling the early vintages of the Mount Pleasant Wine Company. In the succeeding years, she and her husband, Bob, took up residence in the Kansas City area and discovered that other wineries in the state also made enjoyable wines. From this background, she confesses that the much-touted California varietals and the revered European *cuvées* strike her as strange; she prefers the wines of her home state.

The people of Jackson County have a valuable resource in Spring Creek Winery. Located in the southeastern suburb of Blue Springs, the winery stocks of some of the best Missouri wines, many of which are not usually marketed outside of the producing winery. While the McDonalds work through the federal labeling standards that will allow them to release their own Spring de Blanc, a semi-dry fermented apple juice, they

SPRING CREEK Winery, Ltd.
Blue Springs, Missouri

SPRING DE BLANC
MISSOURI TABLE WINE

PRODUCED AND BOTTLED BY SPRING CREEK WINERY, LTD.
BLUE SPRINGS, MO — B.W. MO-158 — CONTAINS SULFITES

recommend prize wines from other Missouri vintners and offering samples in their historic tasting room.

The beauty of the surrounding wine garden and the restored Victorian home that houses their tasting room, gallery, and sunporch attracts almost as much interest from visitors as the wines. Built around 1869, the house once served the practice of Dr. C. C. Frick. In fact, Frick examined his patients in the present-day tasting room. The enclosed wraparound porch was added later, perhaps in the late 1920s. Now tables on the porch provide visitors with a place to eat, after choosing from the Spring Creek Winery's menu of sandwiches and appetizers. With a huge Chinese elm tree for a center piece, the wine garden accommodates up to one hundred people in favorable weather. This capacity, along with room inside for as many as sixty guests, inspires groups to reserve the winery for special occasions, such as wedding receptions, birthday celebrations, and other parties.

Kelly McDonald and her staff share with consumers important information about the quality of Missouri wines. In this one location, tasters can sample the best vintages of Stone Hill, O'Vallon, Les Bourgeois, St. James Winery, and others that the McDonalds have personally selected as the best in Missouri. Visitors to Spring Creek Winery can find the style of wine they prefer before driving across the state in search of this or that vintage.

Bynum Winery

Route 1
13520 South Sam Moore Road
Lone Jack MO 64070   (816) 566-2240

On the Highway 50 corridor that links Kansas City with the Lake of the Ozarks is Lone Jack, Missouri. Two miles east of the point where the solitary jack oak tree once shaded the town's blacksmith shop, the proprietor of Bynum Winery contemplates the future of winemaking in Missouri. From his association with the now-defunct Midi Winery, Floyd Bynum knows first hand about the risks of running a winery and plans accordingly—which often means changing those plans.

He saw seemingly inevitable prosperity at Midi Winery evaporate quickly. In 1982 he started pruning the vines at Midi, which was one of the first wineries to restore the Missouri tradition of winemaking. He eventually took on the responsibilities of winemaker at Midi, serving in that capacity for the last four years of the winery's existence.

With the demise of Midi's vineyards, Bynum almost hesitantly turned his attention to a winery of his own. Located barely west of Johnson County, Bynum Winery posts weekend hours of operation of noon to six o'clock, and whenever his truck is parked in the driveway. Only thirty-some miles from downtown Kansas City on a main route to the Lake of the Ozarks, he wants to reach beyond his tasting room.

Though he expertly plays host and happily pours samples of Bynum wines or a taste from the remaining Midi inventory, he believes Kansas City-area restaurants should provide the appropriate setting for enjoying his wine. He states this belief most directly in his brochure: ''Bynum's philosophy is wine should be savored and enjoyed at meal time and it is not a product to be consumed on the road.''

In addition to an assortment of Midi vintages, Bynum Winery offers wines from dry to sweet made from

French-hybrid grapes, such as Seyval, Chancellor, and Villard Blanc. Vineyards near Knob Noster and Warrensburg supply Bynum with grapes. The winery also ferments the juice of other fruits, such as apples and cherries, when these crops are available.

Weston

North of the I-435 perimeter of Kansas City, the town of Weston has only recently awakened from the nineteenth century. Founded in 1837, Weston grew quickly as a port city on the banks of the Missouri River. Before the Civil War, 5,000 people called Weston their home. In addition to eight churches, two flour mills, and America Bowman's public house (the "oldest brewery west of the Hudson River"), the townsfolk supported a dozen private schools for their children. Steamboats emptied eager pioneers on this landing of the frontier and, for the return trip, stacked their decks with pelts, hemp, and tobacco. The town rivaled Leavenworth and St. Joseph for western commerce; however, its prospects came to an abrupt end in 1857 when, after reaching floodstage, the receding river shrank to a new channel a few miles from Weston's business district.

A century passed without disturbing the town, although tobacco and hemp crops continued to reward the efforts of area farmers. Beginning around 1960, the people of Weston took stock of their community and realized that many pre-Civil War buildings and federal-style mansions stll survived. Suddenly their neglected town took on a stately appearance and the townspeople set about the task of recreating Weston as a thriving city of the early 1850s. Their efforts, beginning on Main Street, were recognized in 1972 with the award of official Historic District status in the National Register of Historic Places. Since then, preservation projects have barely kept apace of public fascination with the antebellum town.

Visitors stroll the length of Main Street, ducking in and out of intriguing lanes, browsing leisurely through the buildings that now sell antiques, crafts, elegant glassware, ice cream, scented soaps and balms, and gourmet cooking equipment. Two Victorian homes with wraparound porches and a federal-style brick building offer charming bed-and-breakfast accommodations that harken back to the days when hospitality was *de rigueur.* The America Bowman Restaurant and O'Malley's 1842 Pub prepare tables with hearty home-cooked fare served on pewterware in the former brewery's barrel-ceilinged cellars. Amid this restoration, two plainly functional tobacco barns of relatively recent construction still store an agricultural product that links the town with its days of glory in the 1850s.

Mission Creek Winery

1099 Welt Street
Weston MO 64098   (816) 386-5770

In the tradition of the centuries-old estates of France, Mission Creek Winery involves the dedication of an entire family. Jim and Joan Keogh returned to Weston from California about fifteen years ago. The family farm, through which Mission Creek runs, was about to change hands, ending the legacy of a hundred-year stewardship of the land. At the time of their return, they may not have envisioned a vineyard on the old homestead; yet, in 1987, joined by their son Jeff and his wife, the Keogh family celebrated its first crush. Through the winter of 1987-88 the members of the family applied their skills and every available off-hour from full-time jobs to build a modern wine-making cellar and attractive tasting room on the north end of Welt Street.

With an allegiance to purity Jeff now says was too strict, the Keoghs bottled their first wine as 100 percent varietals. Since then, however, he has used to his advantage the fifteen percent blend amount allowed by federal regulations in varietal bottling. This margin enables him as a winemaker to improve the bouquet of his Proprietor's Reserve Seyval Blanc, for example, with a small amount of Catawba; or to intensify the color of his Chambourcin with a touch of Baco Noir. In addition to the grapes they cultivate on their ten-acre Mission Creek vineyard, the Keoghs supplement their harvest with grapes grown near the Missouri State Fruit Experiment Station in Mountain Grove, Missouri (see Wine Tour Four).

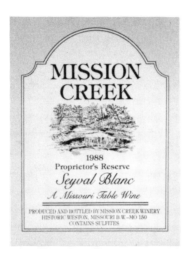

In this learning process, Jeff has veered so far from his initial insistence on varietal purity to apply his skill to proprietary blends, such as Rialto Red, a blend of several red-wine grapes, including some Norton and Chancellor. The unusual name of this wine Jeff attributes to a forgotten shanty town on the Missouri River near Weston. Soon after the founding of Fort Leavenworth in 1820, soldiers looking for a place to relax ''off-base'' patronized the makeshift taverns and gaming rooms of Rialto Landing. In enforcing its policy to keep the soldiers at the fort, the army annexed Rialto and destroyed the flimsy shacks where the soldiers had gathered. By 1854, the town of Leavenworth, Kansas, had sprung up outside the perimeter of the fort to serve the same need that Rialto Landing had once served.

The winery built by Jeff and his parents overlooks Bennett Creek. Though the main room for guests has yet to be finished, the Keoghs have sectioned off a sunny, comfortable corner for a temporary tasting room. Eventually, the main room with the vaulted ceiling will provide ample space to accommodate guests on the busiest of weekends; and a deck overlooking the hilly terrain of the Missouri River valley will enhance the already scenic attraction of the place. Once the Keoghs reach that point in their plans, they will perhaps take a moment to congratulate themselves, perhaps indulge in a glass of the champagne they plan to make; but, the Keoghs are not disposed to easy living. On the heels of this achievement, the family fully expects to begin the expansion of their winery.

Pirtle's Weston Vineyards

P. O. Box 247
502 Spring Street
Weston MO 64098   (816) 386-5588

First located in the America Bowman brewery in the heart of Weston's historic business district, Weston Vineyards found a new home in the German Evangelical Lutheran Church on Spring Street. The 1867 brick building had stood empty for years, its windows the target of stone-throwing vandals, when Elbert and Pat Pirtle envisioned their winery there. Now, among other distinctions, Pirtle's Weston Vineyards claims to be the only Missouri winery to occupy a former church.

With winemaking facilities carried out on ground level, the Pirtles host their tasting counter in the nave of the former church. Once lined with rows of solid pews and strictly devout parishioners, the hall now entertains a revolving retinue of curious visitors to Weston and friends of the winery. From time to time, a group of people will reserve the room for a tasting party of their favorite wines. However, the church has not been completely secularized. As if in tribute to its former life, Pirtle replaced panes of shattered glass in the high-arched casements with stained glass of his own design.

Though striking, the building is but one unique feature of the winery. Since 1980 the Pirtles have made a range of wines, mostly from French hybrid grapes, grown in recent years near Lexington, Missouri. With respect to the previous *Deutsche Evangelisch-Lutherisch Gemeinde*, the Pirtles adopted German names for two of their wines. *Goldeströpfchen* ("droplets of gold") fittingly describes their Vidal table wine. Some aging in oak cooperage endows this wine with the strength of character to stand up to many food accompaniments. The Pirtles' blush wine, called *Rosenblümchen* ("tiny roses"), is primarily Seyval wine, with a small amout of red wine added to impart a tinge of pink to the juice.

The winery also offers a wine blend called Mellow Red, which Elbert Pirtle describes as made from "a cousin of the native Cynthiana grape," that is, Concord. Like other wineries in western Missouri, Weston Vineyards takes advantage of the abundance of locally grown apples to make Missouri Apple Wine. Oak whiskey barrels used for aging this beverage give it an added complexity of flavor beyond hard cider.

Elbert and Pat are most inclined to talk about their mead, an ancient beverage made out of fermented honey. Believed by some to be civilization's first "wine," mead is mentioned in *Beowulf* and early Viking legends as the drink of royalty. In the Middle Ages the people of England considered mead to be an aphrodisiac and thus an appropriate beverage with which to celebrate marriage. According to Pat Pirtle, this function of mead added the word ''honeymoon'' to the English language.

In their mead and wines, the Pirtles respect the long-standing role of wine in important celebrations. To encourage this tradition, they offer special commemorative bottlings of their wine. Kiln-fired and colored, the handmade, clay vessels are distinctively painted and inscribed with a personal message that pertains to the occasion. Like the church itself, these gifts contribute to the unique experience of visiting Pirtle's Weston Vineyards.

MID-MISSOURI

To GENERATIONS OF MISSOURIANS THROUGHOUT the state, Columbia remains forever a special place inhabited by fond memories of college days at ol' Mizzou. For many Missourians, to return to Columbia is to relive the past, or to step physically into a dream. Their eyes refuse to admit any change as they numbly lumber around Jesse Hall and across campus, pan in slow motion through the Strollway, and walk in the dim light cast from Broadway storefronts on Saturday night. Time has stopped.

From one corner of Ninth Street to another, their conversation consists solely of, "That's still here!" and "I remember that!" Occasionally, they will entreat the heavens, "Was that always a frozen yogurt stand?" or "Wasn't there a pizza parlor that had knotty pine paneling? Did the Old Heidelberg have a dinner menu twenty years ago? Didn't Ernie's always serve breakfast on Sunday morning? Did the apartment building on Christian College Avenue ever become as rundown as memory once thought?"

To ask these questions is to challenge the authenticity of a dream. From Nowell's on West Boulevard to Faurot Field, from the rock quarry to the Stephens stables, from Jack's restaurant to the strip pits north of town, from Zesto's on the business loop to the Skyline drive-in, if you don't look too closely, you won't awaken from this reverie.

Les Bourgeois Winery & Bistro

I-70 Exit 115
Rocheport MO 65279   (314) 698-2300

Five miles west of Columbia, a number of attractions

MID-MISSOURI

♦ winery

lure passing travelers to take Exit 115 to Rocheport: the largest open-mouth cave in Missouri, antiques, pony rides, the historic town itself, and the former Pete's Cafe. Before the Bourgeois family moved their winemaking and bottling operations into the empty roadside restaurant, Pete's Cafe had earned local fame for its coffee and square meals. It also earned a place in the *Guinness Book of World Records* for the world's largest rendering of da Vinci's *Last Supper*.

The restaurant had sat idle for several years, and the *Last Supper* had been hauled to a museum when the Bourgeois family discovered in this building enough space to accommodate their huge, upright, stainless-steel fermentation tanks, their newly acquired, Italian-made, state-of-the-art membrane press, and their totally automated bottling line. Although plain and sorely neglected, the shell of Pete's Cafe featured vaulted ceilings and a northern exposure. In addition, the layout of the building allowed the Bourgeois family to consider expanding another concept from the location they had already outgrown in five years of business: the French concept of *le bistro*.

In the summer of 1990 Les Bourgeois Winery & Bistro opened to the public, serving dinner Thursday through Sunday, along with lunch on Sunday. While as a winemaking facility the building is strictly utilitarian, the dining area has emerged with an air of continental Europe smack dab in the middle of Missouri. According to Curtis Bourgeois, the winemaker of the family, the bistro creates an atmosphere for showcasing the food and wine of the region. By this definition, Pete's Cafe was a bistro on the basis of its biscuits and gravy. Now, however, the Bourgeois bistro fetes its guests with soups, such as wild mushroom and greens, light entrees such as grilled monkfish, chicken breasts arranged on beds of fresh red lettuce and radiccio, and award-winning wines vinted from native and French hybrid grapes.

At the linen-covered tables of the bistro, some guests off the interstate might find this menu uncomfortably foreign; yet Curtis knows well his regular clientele. He knows, for example, that Columbia took third place among Missouri cities in liquor sales. While this dubious feat is not surprising for a college town, the city's per capita consumption of wine led every other Missouri city as early as ten years years ago, suggesting a solid base of informed, responsible people who appreciate wine with their meals.

Les Bourgeois Vineyards

P.O. Box 118
Rocheport MO 65279   (314) 698-3401

A mile north of the Rocheport Exit 115 on Route BB, Les Bourgeois staked out its mid-Missouri vineyard site on a high bluff overlooking the Missouri River and the western prairie. From the terraced deck of the wine garden, visitors might imagine that the continental divide lay just over the horizon. The I-70 bridge crosses the river about a mile south of this scenic vista. The Katy Trail, here a ten-mile course connecting Rocheport with McBaine, traces the course of the river, visible through the trees below as a curl of white ribbon.

Dr. Curtis Bourgeois and his family built the winery on the bluff in 1985. He employed the skills of his architect son to design the A-frame tasting room and the multi-level terraces that perch on the edge of the precipice. His son also helped plant the three-acre vineyard that buffers the secluded tasting room from the asphalt road that leads to Rocheport. The younger Curtis took on the mantle of winemaker for the family. He came

by his talent for making wine naturally enough. With family roots that embrace the customs of Cajun Louisiana, Curtis admits that wine often accompanied his family's evening meals. Thus, he learned very early how to appreciate a fine wine. This training developed in him the keeness of palate to distinguish the qualities of a well-made wine. Through study and experience he successfully transferred the sense of his palate to the bouquet and taste of the wines he makes.

He would not boast so; nor would he bring up the awards won by Les Bourgeois. Nonetheless, the judges at the Missouri State Fair two years in a row showed their approval with medals for the winery's off-dry Vidal and its dry Seyval. In terms of sales, patrons of Les Bourgeois vote their liking of Jeunette Rouge, a dry Beaujolais-style red wine made principally from Chancellor grapes, and the semi-sweet Pink Fox, a blend of Seyval Blanc and Catawba.

While most production aspects of the winemaker's craft are now carried on at the bistro, Les Bourgeois still cellars much of its wine at the bluff site. In addition, Bourgeois plans to make a *nouveau*-style Norton from the

1990 harvest of Norton grapes that grow at the bluff. This medium-bodied release, uncharacteristic of other Nortons, aims at a pleasurable fruitiness and softness while in its youth.

To supplement the modest, hand-groomed output of the family's three-acre Rocheport vineyard, Les Bourgeois also leases about forty acres of French hybrids near Advance in southeastern Missouri. At harvest time—an annual period of frenzied activity called "the crush"—refrigerated trucks ferry the whole grapes from the vineyards near Cape Girardeau to the former Pete's Cafe at the Rocheport exit of I-70.

Bristle Ridge Vineyards

P.O. Box 95
Knob Noster MO 65336   (816) 229-0961

Bristle Ridge (pronounce the "t") once served as an advantageous lookout point to the armies of the Civil War. From this hilltop, scouts scanned the flatlands rounded by the Missouri River's loop through the center of the state. Occasionally Ed and Vickie Smith will discover some relic of this conflict—a button, a spur, or a shell casing— as they work in their five-acre vineyard atop Bristle Ridge.

They have worked wine out of this ridge since 1979. According to Vickie, the decision to open a winery came when she "kicked Ed out of the basement," where he had made wine for his entire adult life. At about the same time as this change, they found a slightly listing building perfect for their purposes. Originally intended to serve as a water tower in the 1950s, the simple brick structure remained unfinished until Vickie and Ed saw its potential as a winery.

The second-floor tasting room looks north on the flatlands that Gen. Nathaniel Lyon must have crossed in pursuit of Gen. Sterling Price. As fitting as this vantage point must have been to observe the maneuvers of war, it is an odd place to locate a winery. Sixty-six miles east of Kansas City and 210 miles west of St. Louis on Highway 50, the community of Montserrat's "closest point of reference"—that is, the post office—is Knob Noster, midway between Warrensburg and Sedalia. Like many other towns in old Missouri, Montserrat bustled as an agricultural community in the late 1880s. The prerogative of the railroad, however, isolated the area from the thoroughfares of commerce. Over the decades the town dwindled to a few private residences; the Civil War cemetery, resting ground for both the Blue and the Gray which nearly disappears between the annual mowings; and Whiteman Air Force Base now quarters for warriors trained for conflicts far from the Montserrat life.

The Smiths take pride in producing wine as naturally as possible. Having learned the winemaker's art at the elbow of his uncle, Ed Smith has achieved a unique place for his wines on Missouri's wine map. From the dry Vidal Blanc to the Montserrat Red, a sweet Con-

Bristle Ridge Vineyards

VILLARD NOIR

DRY TABLE WINE

1987

Produced and Bottled by
Bristle Ridge Vineyards, Montserrat, MO
Contains Sulfites   BW-MO-113

cord wine, Bristle Ridge wines have the appeal of old-style country wines. Among the local folk, the water-tower winery overlooking Montserrat is a popular social call. Old gentlemen who drop in the tasting room for a sample and to exchange one-liners with Vickie perhaps remember illegal Prohibition-era wine. It hardly fails that they pack home a couple of bottles under the pickup-truck seat. The fans of Bristle Ridge who buy a couple of cases of hard cider for Christmas gifts are little concerned with fads and fashions of wine determined by the connoisseurs of California and the enophiles of Europe. In other words: they know what they like.

Unfortunately, the limited capacity of Bristle Ridge's vineyards makes its inventory particularly susceptible to depletion as a result of unseasonable weather and the rising interest in its wines. In most years, for example, the Smiths have a de Chaunac wine to offer, as well as a blend based on the Diamond grape. Though now largely forgotten as a wine grape variety in Missouri, the Diamond continues to yield white wine in the northeastern wineries of America. Jacob Moore, an early viticulturist in Brighton, New York, crossed hybrids with native grapes, as well as hybrid pairs, to come up with new varieties such as Moore's Diamond around 1870. In his 1908 *The Grapes of New York*, U.P. Hedrick wrote that in the Diamond:

> The touch of the exotic grape given by the *Vinifera* parents has been just sufficient to give it the richness in flavor of the Old World grape and not overcome the refreshing sprightliness of our native fox grapes. It is without the insipid sweetness of [*vinifera*] or the foxiness of [*labrusca*].

Other wines on the Bristle Ridge wine list include Seyval Blanc, Mont Rose, a blush that uses Rosette grapes, a Burgundy made from Chancellor grapes, and a Villard Noir. The panoramic view invites many visitors to Bristle Ridge to linger at the winery and enjoy a picnic of wine, bread, cheese, and sausage that the Smiths make available. Catawba grape juice is available for children and their parents, too.

Reis Winery

1410 Bagnell Dam Boulevard
Lake Ozark MO 65049   (314) 365-6242

Reis Winery joined ''the strip'' at Lake Ozark in 1990, after twelve years of making wine near Licking, Missouri (see Wine Tour Three—Ozark Highlands). The Reis family chose the Bagnell Dam location for obvious reasons: in the summer months more bumper-to-bumper traffic inches along the Bagnell Dam strip than speeds over Route CC near Maples. While many amusements around the lake stir the youthful energy of any age group, Reis Winery offers adults a less-taxing diversion than go-karts, water slides, miniature golf, and arcade games.

From the winery's deck overlooking Bagnell Dam Boulevard (Business Route 54), parents can dispatch their brood to nearby attractions while they engage in the pursuit of serious relaxation. At the Reis Winery, serious relaxation often demands the exertion of nibbling at cheese wedges and sausage slices, sipping a little wine, and watching the hubbub of the strip with detached curiosity.

In addition to such a peaceful perspective on the American concept of "vacation," Reis Winery offers the full list of wines made at the family's vineyard near Licking. The ten kinds of grape wines and three types of berry wines are joined at the Bagnell Dam tasting counter by two sparkling wines and one bottle-fermented cham-

REIS

MISSOURI

RHINE

White Dinner Wine Produced From Select French Hybrid Grapes Grown at Our Vineyards in the Missouri Ozark Plateau at an Elevation of 1,350 ft.

PRODUCED AND BOTTLED BY
REIS WINERY, BW-MO-108, LICKING, MISSOURI
ALCOHOL 11% BY VOLUME

pagne. The effervescent releases provide many tourists at the lake with the ingredients for marking special occasions—the honeymoon, the birthday, the anniversary.

Bonded in 1990, the winery at Lake Ozark will serve as a tasting room and retail outlet until the Reis family decides on how they want to use their license to make wine there. In the meantime, they will continue to serve samples and host the wine garden deck, introducing vacationers to the estate wines made by Jim's parents, Val and Joy Reis. In addition to wine-related gifts and souvenirs, the winery will make up gift baskets of items chosen from a selection of Missouri's own Morningland Dairy—cheese, sausage, crackers, and, naturally, Missouri wine made at the Reis Winery in the Ozark Highlands viticultural area.

SAINTS OF THE EAST

St. Charles

IN THE LAST TWENTY YEARS, A TRANSFORMATION has taken place on the St. Charles riverfront. Once this town had seemed doomed to become a bland bedroom community of the St. Louis workforce. As affordable, split-level, ranch-style houses took their place on curving streets lined with fast-growing saplings, the riverfront decayed in the midst of empty warehouses and idle factories.

Before mammoth manufacturing industries took over the city, Main Street and Frenchtown had prospered as centers of commerce. St. Charles was known as *Les Petites Côtes* then, after the gently ruffled wedge of land that separated the Mississippi and Missouri rivers.

During Spanish rule, the gates to Louisiana opened slightly to admit a few old-stock Americans, pioneers such as Daniel Boone and family. Boone's quest of the West, the same driving force that led him through the Allegheny Mountains via the Cumberland Gap, guided many of those who crossed the Mississippi River by the Boone's Lick Trail. The first church was named for San Carlos Borromeo, but today, maps depict the town as St. Charles, rather than San Carlos.

After the Louisiana Purchase, adventurers outfitted their westward expeditions there. In 1804 Lewis met Clark at St. Charles, beginning their exploration of the American West. Others who used the town as a starting point included Zebulon M. Pike and Stephen H. Long, whose arrival on the steam-powered *Western Engineer* in 1819 contributed to making St. Charles an important port city. The Americans designated St. Charles as Missouri's first state capital in 1821, an honor it held until 1826.

St. Charles shared with other Missouri River sites the influx of German immigrants in the first half of the nine-

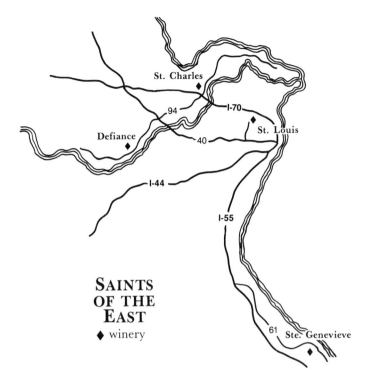

St. Charles

94

I-70

Defiance

40

St. Louis

I-44

I-55

**SAINTS
OF THE
EAST**
♦ winery

61 Ste. Genevieve

teenth century. The arrival of masons, carpenters, and other craftsmen brought to the trading outpost of St. Charles the permanence of a city. Railroads kept the town's industries busy with trade in raw materials and manufactured goods. By the 1870s two-story brick buildings with cast-iron filigree lined both sides of a prosperous Main Street and adjacent streets. Still the cosmopolitan magnet of many cultures, St. Charles in 1874 published five newspapers, three in German.

Twentieth-century economics afflicted St. Charles with a fate that paralleled the plight of many manufacturing centers. The railroads that had superseded river commerce were ignored for the convenience of modern highways. Skilled labor jobs evaporated as manufacturing moved overseas. Far from evolving into a ghost town, however, the city stays alive with transplants from St. Louis who crossed the bridge to escape the presumed decline of that city. Where once the riverfront of St. Charles had thrived with industry, its streets became dangerous, foreboding places visited only by wind-blown debris.

In the 1960s the dilapidated buildings of old St. Charles appeared as blighted eyesores to all but a few visionaries. These people saw through the dark walls of discarded industries and imagined a city in its prime. Over the next twenty years the area underwent radical cosmetic surgery. Once the hulking, windowless factories and warehouses had been removed, sunlight again bathed a core of nineteenth-century buildings fit for a museum. Since then, independent entrepreneurs have embraced the area for its historic value. They shored up and remodeled the old brick structures with an eye to keeping to the original style. A green esplanade sprouted next to the river; and steamboats again tied their lines to the landing, booking passage to the ''good old days.''

The transformation was so complete that all of South Main Street was honored as a historic district. Buildings where tradesfolk once milled grain, sold dry goods, built wagons, barrels, and furniture, now serve gourmet food, sell antiques and old-fashioned novelties, show handicrafts, and provide bed-and-breakfast accommodations. In 1990 a film crew used historic St. Charles as the backdrop for *Return to Hannibal,* a movie about the further adventures of Tom Sawyer and Huckleberry Finn.

Winery of the Little Hills

501 South Main Street
St. Charles MO 63301   (314) 946-9339

Among the prosperous businesses on South Main Street in the late 1800s, Wepprich's Wine Gardens gave the townsfolk of St. Charles a friendly place to socialize. Established in 1859, the winery and its hillside vineyard remained in the Wepprich family until Prohibition closed its doors; for a few years after Repeal, Emil Wepprich struggled to revive the family business. In 1982 Martha Kooyumjian reopened the winery with her husband, Tony. However, her dream of recreating the wine gardens was confined to the basement of the former Wepprich building, now the St. Charles Vintage House. Although she and her husband made wine there, the goal of reestablishing the winery's friendly garden setting had to wait.

A few years passed before Martha caught wind of the availability of a property in the newly revitalized capitol district, several blocks north on Main Street. The turn-of-the-century brick building reflected the charm of the district's former glory. Best of all, it included a vacant lot next door. Because of the adjacent lot, Martha reasoned that this location would make a more suitable setting for a wine garden than the basement of the old Wepprich place.

At first, the building had housed a pharmacy. Later, as the Golden Buffet Tavern, lunch was provided to a draft-beer clientele. With the coming of Prohibition, the premises became a meat locker. One story describes the meat locker as merely a storefront ruse; out of the back door, it was well known then, the proprietor sold whiskey. The repeal of Prohibition ended this dubious enterprise. Once again the building resumed life as a tavern, this time called the Old Golden Buffet. From overgrown bushes in the lot next door, Ben's Barbecue dispensed sandwiches and ribs that won their own local following.

Martha tamed the backyard brambles with brick terraces, wrought-iron tables, and a small gazebo. None of its charm went out with the vines and weeds and brush that, catching wisps of smoke, had cloaked Ben's food with an alluring mystique. With seating for 275 people in the garden, visitors to historic St. Charles find the Winery of the Little Hills to be a relaxing, shaded place to watch the world go by as they enjoy a snack. On weekend evenings, candles light each table and discreetly placed floodlamps revive the memory of what Wepprich's Wine Gardens must have been like. To take advantage of the ambiance, people have reserved this setting for wedding receptions, birthday parties, and other special occasions.

When Nature visits Missouri with the rain and snow of winter, the tasting room becomes a haven from the elements. Martha has succeeded in transferring the comforts of the garden indoors with hanging plants and wide windows facing the street. From 11 A.M. to 6 P.M. Monday through Thursday and until 11 P.M. on Friday and Saturday nights, and from noon until 6 P.M. on Sunday, visitors to the winery may choose from a modest yet appealing menu of appetizers, sandwiches, and desserts. Once her guests have made their selection of food, Martha recommends a trip to the tasting counter where free samples of wine help diners choose a complement to their meal.

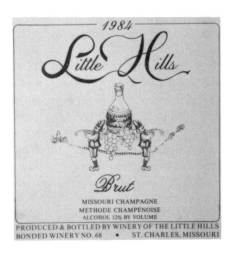

The wine list includes varietals and blends to suit many preferences. The winery's Brut Missouri Champagne, produced in the winery by the *méthode champenoise*, demonstrates Martha's skill as a winemaker. Made to her specifications in Augusta, the Pioneer blend is a favorite semi-dry white wine, while the Chancellor Blanc attracts those who favor a blush, or *blanc de noir*, wine. A new release, *Mon Fils*, also uses Chancellor grapes in a dry, red blend. Wine lovers with a sweet tooth will find satisfaction in the Missouri Valley White, the Missouri Valley Red, or the Spring Rosé.

In addition to a selection of Stone Hill wines, the Winery of the Little Hills also offers its own specialty wines. At different times of the year, these may include the refreshing white May Wine and the aromatic Alpenglow, a spice wine. In the dead of winter, a glass

or mug of warmed Alpenglow, like merrie olde England's
wassail, restores the spirit of the holiday season.

All of the Little Hills wines, which have won fourteen
awards since 1982, are available only at the winery.

Martha also creates made-to-order gift baskets that
match an appropriate Little Hills wine with cheese,
sausage, crackers, or other gourmet treats of choice, such
as Missouri apple butter and jellies.

St. Louis

After the Civil War, with Missouri's wines second only
to California's, St. Louis came to be regarded as a center
of wine research and distribution. As early as 1858
Charles Haven had led a group of investors to form a
commercial vineyard and orchard on a hundred acres
near present-day Rockwoods Reservation in west St.
Louis County. Dr. C. W. Spalding, a physician, established the Cliff Cave Wine Company near the intersection of Baumgartner and Telegraph roads in south St.
Louis County, which produced 3,000 gallons in 1869.
In October 1870 Cliff Cave won the Best Norton diploma
at the St. Louis Fair. In regional competitions sponsored
by the Missouri Horticultural Society, J. J. Kelly of
Webster Groves won recognition for his White Concord,
judged as "the best of all Concords on exhibition new
or old." Another Webster Groves vintner, E. R. Mason,
received the best rating for his 1868 Norton.

In Florissant the St. Stanislaus seminary, now a
museum of the Jesuit province, vinted sacramental wine
for religious institutions throughout the Midwest as well
as commercial wine for sale to the general public and
won a medal at the 1904 World's Fair. Isaac Cook's
American Wine Company shipped Cook's Imperial Brut
sparkling wine to eager customers world wide. From
Bushberg, in Jefferson County, Isidor Bush & Son &
Meissner supplied vineyards with coveted pest-resistant
rootstock and won international awards for the wine it
made at its St. Louis winery.

This tremendous potential of winemaking in St. Louis
was enhanced by the contributions a number of prominent scientists, horticulturists, and entrepreneurs in the

second half of the nineteenth century. For example, George Engelmann, who had emigrated to America in 1832 after earning a medical degree from the University of Würzburg, carried out an extensive botanical classification of native grapes. Though his immediate fame came as a St. Louis physician, his contribution to viticulture lived long after him. Through his friendship with Henry Shaw, Engelmann helped to shape the purpose and mission of the first public botanical garden in the United States. His influence elevated Shaw's Garden from an attractive botanical park to a scientific research insitution. As a part of this legacy, the Missouri Botanical Garden today boasts a herbarium of nearly four million plant species collected since the early eighteenth century.

Bardenheier's Wine Cellars

1019 Skinker Parkway
St. Louis MO 63112   (314) 862-1400

In 1873 John Bardenheier, a recent immigrant from Oberlanstein, Germany, established the John Bardenheier Wine and Liquor Company. Its solid reputation as an importer of European wine allowed the firm to expand into production and bottling. At first it used grapes grown in Hermann; later it also vinified grapes from California and Ohio to stock its massive cellars on lower Market Street.

The firm stayed in the Bardenheier family for one hundred ten years. Operating longer than any other winery in Missouri, Bardenheier's interrupted winemaking only during Prohibition. It again became bonded as a winery in 1933 at a new location. Early plans for a national park in downtown St. Louis, now the Jefferson National Expansion Memorial, brought about Bardenheier's move to the vacant streetcar terminus on Skinker Parkway. Track fragments of the former trolley line still run aimlessly through parts of the winery.

In the 1970s and early 1980s Bardenheier's briefly returned to making a premium line of varietal wine from Missouri-grown hybrid grapes: Chelois, Maréchal Foch, Seyval, and Vidal. Grapes for the Chateau Thayer label wine came from a sixty-five-acre vineyard in southern Missouri.

In 1983 Futura Coatings of Hazelwood, Missouri, acquired Bardenheier's Wine Cellars. Futura's president, E. Dean Jarboe, had become acquainted with the wine industry by developing an exterior foam coating to insulate wine fermentation and storage tanks.

Today Bardenheier's continues to produce and sell more wine than any other Missouri winery, annually approaching the one million gallon mark. Its selection of Sherry, Port, Vermouth, and cordials comprises the company's best-known products. With natural fruit flavors added to blended white wine, its Amanté Wine Coolers come in Raspberry, Wildberry Plus, Passion Tyme, and Premium White flavors. The firm also makes a fortified red grape juice, Rosie O'Grady, its Old Time Hard Cider, an Old Fashion Concord, and a alcohol-free Ozark Mountain Catawba Juice from its Thayer, Missouri, vineyard. In 1991, the firm will debut a bottled effervescent water with the label Spumante Spring.

Defiance

Thirty miles west of St. Louis, Highway 94 turns hard across the former rail bed of the Missouri, Kansas & Texas tracks. Defiance, Missouri, located in an abrupt jog in the road, is made up of a hair-styling salon, a used tractor lot, a couple of good-time taverns, two austere clapboard churches, and an antique store, which spills its contents onto a long plank porch. In the days of the railroad's progress through St. Charles County, the community vied with nearby Matson for a whistle stop. Its residents battled tenaciously against the Matson depot, won, and named their town Defiance to reflect their victory.

Whether the Z-turn existed before the town or vice versa matters little now as Defiance, true to its name, would never allow a straightening of the route that would let passersby coast on by.

Not far from Defiance, Daniel Boone ended his days in his son's cabin. Until their remains were repatriated to Kentucky, Dan'l and his beloved Rebecca rested here.

Boone Country Winery

125 Boone Country Lane
Defiance MO 63341 (314) 987-2400

Just west of the town of Defiance, a steep hillside rises from the Katy Trail and overlooks the broad Missouri River valley. The first members of the Wissmann family settled here in the late 1800s, when the farms along both sides of the Missouri River harbored a strongly German community. Then, the river ran in a channel much closer to the Wissmann's farm than it does today. Above the fickle river, which brought flood waters to the foot of Boone Country Lane and submerged the defunct railbed as late as 1986, four generations of the Wissmann family have tilled this ridge.

In 1982 the Wissmanns turned a twelve-acre tract of the family farm into a vineyard and converted the front parlor of the family's Victorian house into a tasting room. In 1985 they opened Boone Country Winery. Not to be confused with Boone's Farm, Boone Country Winery makes a modest selection of grape-based wines that includes several vintages flavored with berry juice concentrate. All the grapes that go into making their wine are grown in sight of the winery itself. Mainly planted in Vidal and Delaware grapes, the vineyard also supports Niagara and Concord vines. From these grapes comes the full selection of Boone Country Winery wines, estate grown, produced, and bottled.

Carol Wissmann offhandedly advises visitors to "drink the wine you enjoy." Best sellers at Boone Country Winery include a semi-dry blend of Vidal and Delaware called Boone Country White and the sweet, raspberry-flavored Raspberry Patch. Their semi-dry Blush earns a unique distinction by using pink Delaware grapes. At opposing ends of the taste spectrum, the Wissmann's Old Fashioned Grape claims to be "just like what grand-dad used to make," that is, a sweet Concord wine, while the St. Charles County Vidal, a new release in 1990, appeals to dry-wine tastes.

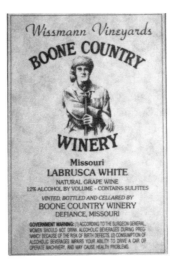

As cycling enthusiasts and hikers discover the Katy Trail, more visitors take the hill to the winery. Once there, with bicycles propped against the winery's picket fence, they might choose to quench their thirst with a refreshing berry-flavored wine such as Peach Hollow, Strawberry Fields, or Blackberry Thicket. Those who have also worked up an appetite will find a selection of cheese, sausage, and snacks available for purchase to enjoy on the picnic grounds.

From April through October, Boone Country Winery hosts evenings of music on the last Sunday of each month. Like the wines, the entertainers represent a selection to please any preference from polka to Dixieland jazz. An ornate gazebo on the winery's grounds becomes a band-stand on these occasions.

The tasting room offers a unique assortment of wine-related souvenirs—Carol's grapevine wreaths and homemade wine-grape jellies, and hand-crafted ornaments, dolls, and decorations. For holidays and special occasions, the winery also creates made-to-order gift boxes and baskets.

Ste. Genevieve

A trip to Ste. Genevieve, Missouri's oldest permanent settlement, presents an opportunity to experience Upper Louisiana's French heritage. Established about 1749, the frontier outpost acquired the look of a town in 1763 when British occupation of the east bank of the Mississippi Valley drove more French settlers across the Mississippi River from Kaskaskia. The rich floodplain on the west bank looked promising for agriculture, but the French also wanted to live under the jurisdiction of the Roman Catholic government of Spain rather than England's Anglicans.

Residents abandoned the original site of their town after the great flood of 1785, taking the high ground around *La Petite Rivière Gabouri*, from which the present-day city grew. The French laid out their community with a great field, *le grand champ*, on the rich bottomland next to the river. Characteristic of agriculture in France, individual families worked long narrow strips of the field while livestock shared pasture in nearby common fields. Their homes also made a lasting impression on the character of the eighteenth-century town. They formed their exterior walls by setting logs vertically into the ground, the *poteaux-en-terre* style of the frontier French. Roofs overlapped the walls in many instances, creating long porches, called *galeries*.

In 1796 Jean Jacques Dufour, a Swiss citizen, investigated the Mississippi Valley between St. Louis and the mouth of the Ohio River for the potential location of his *Fiersnewyard*, or "First Vineyard." On hearing that the Jesuit mission at Kaskaskia cultivated grapes for making sacramental wine, Dufour journeyed to that place across the river from Ste. Genevieve. He found only the vestiges of a garden forsaken by the Jesuits, leading Dufour to speculate that Kaskaskia viniculture "had not been so successful as represented to me; but had been subject to the same sickness which afflicts now all imported grapes ..." He also learned that the French government had discouraged winemaking "for fear the culture of the grapes should spread in America and hurt the wine trade of France."

Farming was the principal occupation, but fur trading, salt extraction on Saline Creek, and lead mining at Mine La Motte also occupied the energies of the original settlers of Ste. Genevieve. Such endeavors tended to attract a shifting populace of entrepreneurs, hired workers, and *coureurs de bois* to the town. For the most part these people lived in carefree isolation, enjoying their Roman Catholic customs, their fêtes, and their French heritage until long after the Louisiana Purchase.

The rich land of the common field did not require careful cultivation to supply the early Ste. Genevieve residents with their everyday food needs. When Henry Marie Brackenridge visited the town in 1810 and 1811, he noted that winemaking had been "at present almost neglected." Here, though, as in other parts of the state, wild grapes grew extensively. In addition to the winter grape (possibly *Vitis cordifolia*) that had gone into the earliest local vintages, Brackenridge's *Views of Louisiana*, published in 1814, recorded specimens of *Vitis aestivalis*, the summer grape, and *Vitis riparia*, the river grape, in the area. To Brackenridge's palate, the local wine did not live up to the reputation accorded it by previous visitors.

By the time of Missouri's statehood, Ste. Genevieve had received many immigrants from southern Germany, particularly Roman Catholics who wanted to escape the tide of Lutheranism in their homeland. The Germans reshaped the town by building brick businesses and homes with gabled roofs. Their choice of building material contributed a permanence to the community that permitted the cultivation of grapes, a pursuit that from planting could take as long as four years to yield a harvest of wine.

In 1849, as interest in viniculture spread among German communities throughout the state, the *Western Journal and Civilian* of St. Louis reported that "there are some vineyards near St[e]. Genevieve, and some very good hock has been received here from Mr. Root, of that place." The term "hock" referred to Hochheim, Germany, a Rhine valley town west of Frankfurt. In general, Hochheim's Riesling grapes were harvested late with a concentrated sugar content. Such shriveled grapes made the hock of the Rhinegau, an intensely sweet wine balanced by characteristic flowery and spicy overtones.

These days, Ste. Genevieve literally revels in its history. Bastille Days are celebrated in mid-July. *Jour de Fête*, which takes place on the second full weekend of August, has for twenty-five years brought craft and food booths to downtown streets in a celebration of pioneer arts and industry. The first weekend in October recognizes the German contribution to the city, coinciding with the grape harvest. French Colonial Days are celebrated on the first weekend in November; and for the Old Country Christmas Walk, downtown dons yuletide decorations of Christmas past.

One of the favorite customs of Ste. Genevieve, *La Guignolée,* gives a special flavor to the New Year's Eve observance. In this tradition, a band of costumed men parades the streets from home to home. To the residents they encounter, they sing *La Guignolée.* Through several verses, the singers ask first for the listener's money; when not a *sou* is delivered, they entreat the householders to give up a daughter; when the *mademoiselle* comes not forth, a drink or a snack sends them on their way. The *bon hommes* of Ste. Genevieve have performed this ritual since the days when France reigned on the west bank of the Mississippi.

Sainte Genevieve Winery

245 Merchant Street
Ste. Genevieve MO 63670   (314) 883-2800

and the vineyard ...

Highways C & EE
Route 3, Box 384
Ste. Genevieve MO 63670   (314) 483-2012

Not surprisingly, the Ste. Genevieve "hock" of today comes from the winery of the Hoffmeisters, Linus and Hope. Starting as wine hobbyists in the 1960s, the Hoffmeisters planted their first vineyard in 1978. Success in growing their own French hybrid grapes on the "farm" northwest of Ste. Genevieve led them to open their first winery in 1984. In addition to their own four-acre vineyard, Linus began tending the arbors of neighbors for a share of the harvest and buying grapes from other growers in Missouri.

The Hoffmeisters again expanded their "hobby" by setting up a second bonded winery and tasting room in Ste. Genevieve's French Colonial Historic District. Located in a 5,000 square foot, fourteen-room, turn-of-the-century residence, the newest Sainte Genevieve Winery added an important resource to the Hoffmeister's business: a capacious, high-ceiling cellar with a year-round temperature of between sixty and seventy degrees Fahrenheit.

Though this feature is important to the wine sampled in the first-floor tasting room, the attention of visitors might tend to focus on the tall pocket doors to the dining room, the French doors with the original imperfect glass of hand manufacture, and, on special occasions, a host and hostess in colonial dress. The Hoffmeisters, like many of the people who live in Ste. Genevieve, enjoy acting out roles in the city's historical events.

Sainte Genevieve Winery white wines range from the dry Vidal to the dessert-style Amoureaux. Other white wines include the oak-aged, semi-dry Ste. Gemme, named for Jean Baptiste Saint Jeme Beauvais who settled here in 1754, and the Seyval Blanc, a uniquely sweet style of this hybrid. In red wines, the winery features the dry, fruity Beauvais, the semi-dry Bolduc, in which a bit of Norton adds complexity and some aging potential, and the ubiquitous Missouri wine, sweet Concord. In addition to these vintages, the winery released a selection of non-grape juice wines in 1990, including apple, cherry, red raspberry, and blackberry.

By previous arrangement, wine lovers still have the opportunity to see the winemaking process, from vine to fermented wine, at the Sainte Genevieve Winery ''farm,'' about twenty miles from downtown. The Hoffmeisters recommend calling the farm to schedule a leisurely visit in the country. Nearby Hawn State Park and Bonne Terre Mines are also points of interest.

When Linus and Hope Hoffmeister began bringing their family to Ste. Genevieve for summer vacation, they fell in love with the town. Today their love has matured into a deep, warm relationship with ''Ste. Gen's'' past. While they take pride in their wine, they hope that visitors to their winery will also be smitten with the enchantment of this special place.

GRAPES
INTO
WINE

If nature furnishes me in the grapes which I intend to make into wine, a juice which contains everything to make first-class wine, in the right proportions, I shall leave it so on the principle, "let well enough alone;" but if I think there are deficiencies which can be supplied by adding to that which is already in the must, but not in sufficient quantity, I shall do so, as my reason was given me by an All-wise Creator for the purpose of using it to the best advantage.

George Husmann
Report of the Commissioner of Agriculture for the Year 1867

NATURE MAKES THE WINE AND MORTALS MAKE the bottle. Nature provides all the necessary components to ferment grape juice in the fruit hanging on the vine. Ripe grapes need only be gathered into a container of some kind for spontaneous fermentation to take place. Historians trace the origins of wine to ancient times when berries, nuts, and herbs of forest and meadow were stored. Omar Khayyam, the twelfth-century Persian poet, fashioned one version of the story in the *Rubaiyat*. At the royal court of Persia, servants stored grapes in urns for snacking. In one urn that had been put aside, the grapes bubbled and smelled strange. Thinking the substance to be poisonous, a young woman seeking to end her life of constant headaches drank the juice of the ''spoiled'' grapes. The wine put her to sleep, a sleep from which she woke feeling unusually refreshed. Thus, according to Khayyam's tale, began the dual role of fermented grape juice as a relaxing libation and as a medicinal tonic.

Since that legendary time, human ingenuity has refined the process to guide nature toward a predictable, consistent result. Today's winemakers harvest their grapes when the juice has reached a sugar content of twenty to twenty-four percent. At this point, the grapes contain enough sugar to yield an alcohol content of ten to twelve percent, sufficient to preserve them. Ideally, the sugar and acidity of harvested grapes already exists in the proper proportions to make wine, or as close to those proportions as the variety will ever develop in the given climate and soil conditions. The winemaker hauls the grapes to the winery and feeds them through a crushing machine that breaks the skin and removes the stems. Once the skins of the grapes split, the juice becomes vulnerable to yeasts that have colonized the chalky film, called ''bloom,'' on the surface of the grape. Almost immediately, the yeast begins to interact with the sugar of the juice, secreting an enzyme that converts the sugar into equal amouts of alcohol and carbon dioxide.

A BREAKTHROUGH

A breakthrough in understanding and controlling this process came in 1857 when Louis Pasteur, at the behest of Napoleon III, demonstrated the role of yeast in making wine. As a facultative anaerobe, that is, one capable of living with or without oxygen, yeast cells multiply slowly in the absence of oxygen, while efficiently converting sugar to alcohol and carbon dioxide. In an oxygen-rich environment, however, yeast grows quickly, producing mainly carbon dioxide. Yeast continues to secrete enzymes until all the sugar has been converted or until the alcohol content of the juice reaches a level of ten to fourteen percent, the point at which yeast can no longer survive. Other factors, such as temperature extremes, can also arrest the action of the yeast.

Thus, the winemaker's role at this stage is to facilitate the start of yeast growth, to sustain the fermentation by controlling the temperature, and to decide when to curtail the activity of the yeast cells. In a dry wine, the winemaker allows all the sugar to be converted into alcohol; varying shades of sweetness are possible by ending the yeast's activity while some sugar remains in the juice.

Since the time of Pasteur, winemakers have also had the option of selecting the particular kind of yeast they want to carry out the fermentation. Sulfur dioxide, long used as a disinfectant of wine casks, eliminates undesirable bacteria that appear naturally on the skin of the grapes. Powdered potassium metabisulphites, ''sulfites,'' preserve the wine from the oxidation that causes browning and gives it an unpleasant "burnt" taste. Winemakers also use "meta" as a dry scouring powder to remove grape stains from their hands and as an agent to arrest fermentation before all the sugar has been converted to alcohol. Starting with "clean" juice, the winemaker can select the strain of yeast to carry out the fermentation process. Either purchased for the purpose of making wine or cultured from wild organisms that survived the dose of meta, a yeast-cell line can be preserved and used year after year (like sourdough bread starter) from refrigerated cultures.

Through this basic procedure, the winemaker, like a concerned parent, guides the wine to a bright future. Also as in childrearing, in winemaking there are no guarantees of success. Occuring as naturally as wine does, vinegar results when not enough alcohol is created to dominate the oxygen. Even after fermentation has ended successfully, oxygen can stir the formation of vinegar. In the process of pasteurization, a liquid (for example, wine or milk) is heated enough to kill the vinegar bacteria without harming the heat-resistant spores that carry out fermentation. As any parent knows, the path to maturity is frought with perils; yet a troubled childhood does not necessarily lead to maladjusted adulthood, and the perfect child can, for reasons unknown, grow up to be a social misfit. In bringing the wine to maturity, the winemaker does the best job possible with the available materials, tools, and environment.

WHITE WINE

Once crushed, white-wine grapes take a different route from red-wine grapes. To make white wine, the winemaker presses the juice from the stems, skins, and pulp, leaving a cake of solid matter called the marc or pomace. Most often the marc returns to the earth as cattle feed or vineyard fertilizer. However, in some places the marc is distilled to make cheap brandy or, as in Italy, a liqueur called *grappa*.

The press juice, called "must," flows to a fermentation vat, usually a stainless steel tank. During the period of primary fermentation, perhaps several weeks for a white wine, the winemaker pays close attention to the temperature of the vat and to the rising content of alcohol. When the level of sugar falls to the desired point, the wine is siphoned from the fermentation vat, leaving behind dead yeast cells and other solids, called the lees. The winemaker may ''rack'' the wine in this way several times to achieve as clear a product as possible. Eventually, white wine ends up in storage tanks, sometimes small oak barrels, before it is bottled.

SPARKLING WINE

From the white wine's fermentation vat, the winemaker can guide the wine toward an effervescent destiny, by one of three methods of making sparkling wine. *Méthode champenoise*, the process used by wineries in the Champagne district of France, produces the finest grade of sparkling wine. Adopted by the makers of fine champagne in Missouri, the process involves bottling the wine before fermentation has ceased. The bottles, constructed of heavier glass than still-wine bottles, are stored neck down. Every few days, a winery employee (the *remueur*, in France) turns every bottle with a twist of the wrist. The dent in the bottom of the champagne bottle aids the grip for this job of *remuage*, or ''riddling.'' The slight and regular agitation forces dead yeast cells and other solids into the neck of the bottle. Riddling continues for a month or more, until all the sediment has collected in the neck of the bottle. Prior to shipment, the necks of the bottles are frozen, the bottles are opened, and the ice plug of sediment shoots out. The bottle is quickly corked and wired and set aside to rest. The label of champagne made in this fashion will display the phrase *méthode champenoise* or ''fermented in *this* bottle.''

In the transfer process, the wine is fermented in a bottle, but not the bottle that ends up on the grocery-store shelf. Rather, the individually bottled wine is emptied into a vat at the end of fermentation, where in bulk, the wine is filtered and processed before going back into the bottles that will be sold to the customer. An even quicker method, the bulk or ''charmat'' process ferments wine in a large tank, putting off individual bottling until the wine has finished its fermentation and it has been filtered and processed.

RED WINE

To make red wine, the crushed red grapes stay in contact with the skins for a period of days. As fermentation of the juice begins to take place, the alcohol extracts valuable components from the skins, particularly pigments, aromatic elements, and acids. Ordinarily, the juice of any grape runs clear. Blush and red wines gain their tint by contact with the skins. While color and aroma are important aesthetic attributes of a fine wine, acids in the skins serve a useful purpose.

Tannin, the main acid component, gives wine its astringent feel in the mouth, comparable in the extreme to the sensation of a velvet or felt coating on the tongue and teeth. While the astringency of tannin imparts a degree of complexity to the taste of wine, helping to balance the taste of fruit and the alcohol, the acid also helps to settle out particulate matter and to inhibit bacterial growth. Excellent red wines will tend to taste hard and astringent when young; with age, however, the tannin softens to an equal footing with the fruit and alcohol of the wine's overall presence.

Malic acid also plays an important role in softening a young wine's astringency in a secondary fermentation process. Once the primary fermentation process has ended, or nearly so, the wine is separated from the lees and pumped to another storage vat, where secondary fermentation—either intentionally or unintentionally—often takes place. In malolactic fermentation, bacteria in the wine feed on malic acid, converting it to soft lactic acid. This process reduces the total acidity of wine, an aid to winemakers in Burgundy, the Rhine valley, and Missouri where cool climates usually produce high-acid grapes. Occasionally, the happy accident of malolactic fermentation brings a light carbonation to wine. Uncontrolled, however, the process can saturate bottled wine with trapped carbon dioxide, making it muddled or gaseous.

During the red wine's initial fermentation, it bubbles violently and gives off heat. Carbon dioxide pushes the skins to the top of the fermentation tank, forming a solid crust over the wine that the French call the *chapeau*. To keep fermentation from stalling, the winemaker punches down this cap of skins or pumps juice over the top of it. This action aerates the juice, promoting the growth of yeast. At the conclusion of fermentation, the cap sinks and the wine is removed from the marc and stored in closed vats or barrels. Over the next few months, the red wine is periodically racked, that is, separated from sediment that has collected in the bottom of the container, before being pumped into bottles.

BEAUJOLAIS NOUVEAU

While many adjustable variables in the winemaking process allow the winemaker to apply personal judgment and craft and to guide the wine toward its destiny, the essentials of the process do not differ from one region to another. However, a major deviation from the usual procedure characterizes a style of wine from the Beaujolais region of southern Burgundy. In November each year wine lovers worldwide eagerly anticipate the arrival of *Beaujolais nouveau*, the first bottling of the current year's Gamay vintage. Not intended to be cellared, this wine quickly matures to lightness and simplicity through carbonic maceration. In carbonic maceration, the winemaker bypasses the crushing machine and loads whole bunches of grapes into a primary fermentation tank. The sheer weight of the grapes breaks some of the skins, and most of the fermentation takes place inside the individual grapes. After a few days, the wine is drained from the marc and allowed to continue fermentation separately. Within weeks, the vintage is ready to be bottled and sent around the world to wine drinkers who look forward to *Nouveau* Day like baseball fans waiting for the first news of spring training.

Missouri winemakers have also experimented with carbonic maceration to produce Beaujolais-style wine. The main goal in applying carbonic maceration to making red wine in Missouri is to control acids. Similar to northern France and Germany, the relatively short growing season of Missouri yields grapes with high acid content and low sugar development. In such parts of the winemaking world, winemakers not infrequently add sugar to insure that the yeast has enough raw material with which to produce an amount of alcohol sufficient to preserve and stabilize the wine.

The sugaring process is called "chaptalization" after Jean-Antoine Chaptal, Napoleon's minister of the interior, who, in 1801 proposed this solution to the frequent condition of underripe grapes. In California, where a long growing season can bring grapes past their optimum point of ripeness, chaptalization is strictly against the law unless the winemaker adds concentrated grape juice. At the same time, the high sugar of California grapes typically accompanies a low acid content, which makes secondary malolactic fermentation an unpleasant condition. To counteract low acid content, the winemakers of California often boost the wine's tartaric acid and add more sulfur dioxide to stabilize and preserve the vintage.

THE CRAFT OF WINEMAKING

A winery tour at any time of the year will likely catch one or another aspect of this process in action. Like other forms of agriculture, the cycle of growing wine follows the seasons. From the winter pruning of the vines, to selecting the spring's new shoots that will bear the summer's fruit, to the autumn crush, and finally, guiding the wine through infancy to maturity, the *vigneron's* work alternates between growing, processing, and marketing the wine. Few other industries of this scale carry out all these functions at the same site. It its way, winemaking is a craft, overseen by the artist from conception to the selection of materials to the execution and shaping of the final piece.

One of the features of the wineries' calendar is contact with the public. Every day the winemaker pours samples of recent releases and receives an immediate evaluation. Without exception Missouri winemakers enjoy entertaining visitors, whether introducing curious newcomers to the world of wine or revealing insights about their craft to knowledgeable connoisseurs.

Tasting rooms present a list of wines from dry to sweet. Unless one has a penchant for a particular style of wine or varietal, tasting generally proceeds in that order. Even at the home dinner table, the order of enjoying wine follows this basic pattern, with the sweet wines usually saved for dessert. Once diners learn to appreciate the dry wines, such as dry Seyval Blanc with sauteed chicken breasts, Villard Noir with barbecued pork steaks, or an off-dry Vignoles with smoked turkey, they might find that sweet wines also have their place on the menu.

THREE SIMPLE RULES

Although many wine experts suggest enjoying wine through a complicated code of etiquette, only three rules really matter:

1) Hard liquor impairs the taste buds for appreciating the subtleties of wine.
2) Choose the wines you enjoy.
3) Enjoy the wines you choose.

The only drawback to Missouri wines is the absence of *vin ordinaire* from grocery-store shelves. *Vin ordinaire* is that type of wine defined as reasonable in cost, enjoyable to drink, and readily available. Missouri wines are all extra-*ordinaire*, due to their limited distribution.

In specialty liquor stores, meanwhile, the consumer might find a few premium varietals and blends. Only when the number and output of Missouri wineries increase will the consumer in St. Louis or Kansas City have the luxury of purchasing at everyday prices the wide variety of Missouri wines. Consumers must share the for this condition with state and federal legislators. Only through consumers' increased awareness will *vin ordinaire* become routinely available in grocery stores where Missourians obtain other foods of the table.

Nearly two hundred years ago, Thomas Jefferson commented on this problem in America in a letter to one M. de Neville:

> It is an error to view a tax on [wine] as merely a tax on the rich. It is a prohibition of its use to the middling class of our citizens and a condemnation of them to the poison of whisky, which is desolating their houses. No nation is drunken where wine is cheap; and none sober where the dearness of wine substitutes ardent spirits as the common beverage. It is, in truth, the only antidote to the bane of whisky.

GRAPES
OF
MISSOURI

U NTIL THE DISCOVERY OF THE NEW WORLD, European winegrowers knew of only one species of wine grapes, the classic varieties of *Vitis vinifera* ("wine bearing"). While the first explorers to cross the Atlantic Ocean found wild grapes growing in abundance, none of the plants appeared identical to *vinifera*. Along with such exotic botanical specimens as potatoes, tomatoes, corn, and tobacco, the new grape types challenged the knowledge of sixteenth-century botantists. Of the known *Vitis* species, generally agreed to be somewhat fewer than sixty, more than half originated in North America.

NEW WORLD GRAPES

Almost from the outset, the Europeans arriving in the Western Hemisphere attempted to vinify the strange new grapes that easily slipped free of their tough skins. By the broadest definition, the fruit made wine, or, at least, a drink enough like wine to suitably accompany the first Thanksgiving dinner. But the taste reminded the colonists of no wine they had enjoyed in Europe. When crushed, these grapes gave off a pungent aroma described as "foxy." For some writers of the time the term simply meant "wild." Others used the word to compare the odor to an animal's wet fur. Over time, however, foxy came to mean any strongly foreign taste or smell of wine, including an overpowering flavor of the grape. Many distinct species and varieties from different locales acquired the designation "fox grapes," that is, grapes without a *vinifera* pedigree.

Attempts by settlers to cultivate imported varieties failed to an even greater degree than the dismal trials with native grapes. Occasionally, the classic vines from Europe made it to their third year and began to yield fruit. Virtually none matured to full-bearing age. The colonists correctly attributed the failure of *Vitis vinifera* to the severity of the winter weather. Mysterious pests and unknown plant diseases also decimated the fragile vines.

As a result of the colonists' efforts to cultivate both

European and native species, the short-lived *vinifera* made an indelible mark on American plants. Through chance pollenation with European grapes, the native plants changed. This evolutionary accident did not suddenly render the native species suitable for making palatable wine; yet nearly all of the native species lost some of their original characteristics.

Centuries before, *Vitis vinifera* had undergone similar changes as it moved out of its original home around Greece and intermingled with the wild vines of Europe. Like their counterparts in the New World, the *vinifera* of old evolved into winemaking varieties in three ways: through cross-pollenation (either natural or technological); through cuttings which exactly duplicated the qualities of a desired variety; or, less often, through bud mutation which could be perpetuated by cuttings.

Like their American cousins, the wild species bore either male or female flowers. In these plants only the female bore fruit after being pollenated by the male. The resulting seeds unpredictably inherited some characteristics from each parent. A few plants, however, exhibited both male and female reproductive organs in their flowers, a characteristic that botantists called "perfect." Because their seeds remained true clones of one, self-pollenating parent, these plants were selected to propagate distinct winegrowing varieties.

In the New World, grape varieties born of the chance pollenation of *vinifera* and native species retained their original classifications, such as *Vitis labrusca, Vitis riparia, Vitis rotundifolia,* and *Vitis aestavalis.* Thus, when the viticulturists of the eighteenth and nineteenth centuries discussed American grapes, they referred to varieties improved by pollenation with *vinifera.*

The Alexander grape, for instance, became the first such variety to exhibit potential for producing commercial-quality wine. Believed to be the Constantina grape, a variety of *Vitis vinifera* from the Cape of Good Hope, it was called the "Cape grape." In having both male and female flower components, the Alexander possessed traits of its cultivated *vinifera* parent.

As Gottfried Duden traveled down the Ohio River in 1826, he sampled wine of the Alexander grape at the

Dufours' settlement in Vevay, Indiana. Duden's negative evaluation foreshadowed the end of cultivation of the Alexander grape in America. More than Duden's remarks, the discovery of Catawba and Concord varieties brought about the Alexander's fall in popularity as a wine grape.

Many other domestic grape varieties were classified as native to the New World, such as the Isabella and the Delaware; yet, each of these varieties—even Concord and Catawba—became a promising wine grape only through accidental contact with *vinifera* pollen. For that reason, many wine experts through the years categorically dismissed the wine potential of true native species. With few exceptions, no true species existed unchanged after the arrival of the Europeans.

In Missouri, as in many other parts of America, viticulturists grow three main categories of grapes: *Vitis vinifera*, the wine-bearing vine of Europe; native varieties, which evolved through chance pollenation; and, hybrids developed through intentional cross breeding programs of the nineteenth and twentieth centuries.

VITIS VINIFERA VARIETIES

Though early American viticulturists labored doggedly to transplant *vinifera* from Europe to the New World, the fragility of these varieties made their cultivation east of the Rockies all but impossible. Outside the favored California climate, dashed hopes marked every chapter in the first two hundred years of winegrowing history in the Western hemisphere. *Vinifera* vines in the eastern states seemed as tenuous as orchids in Antarctica. With the success of native varieties in the mid-nineteenth century, followed by the development of hardy hybrids, attempts to cultivate *vinifera* ceased for the most part in vineyards east of the Rockies.

In 1950 Dr. Konstantin Frank changed the prevailing attitude about growing *vinifera* in the eastern states. Frank came to the United States as a refugee from Germany and started work at Gold Seal Vineyards of Hammondsport, in the Finger Lakes district of New York. Drawing on his extensive experience growing *vinifera* in

Russia, Frank became the leading proponent of the suitability of these varieties in vineyards east of the Rockies. Through the use of new agricultural chemicals, conscientious site selection, and vineyard management practices, Frank disproved the experience of three hundred years of failure to grow *vinifera* in the eastern United States. Very vocal in his criticism of wine made from hybrids or native grapes, Frank released his own first vintage, a late-harvest Johannisberg Riesling, in 1962.

The success of Frank's innovative vineyard techniques led winegrowers in other states, including Missouri, to consider planting *vinifera*. In the almost- three-decade span since Frank's Riesling, further advances in agricultural chemistry have improved the outlook for growing *vinifera* in the eastern states. While not definitive or exhaustive, the following list describes the principal *vinifera* grapes cultivated in Missouri. Other *vinifera* not to be overlooked by even the casual wine lover include: Sauvignon Blanc, the chief white-wine grape of Bordeaux; Chenin Blanc, France's Loire valley white-wine grape; Gewürztraminer, a pungent and spicy pink grape vinted successfully in Alsace and California; Gamay, the grape of every November's *Beaujolais Nouveau*; the Rhône valley's Syrah (called Petit Syrah in California); and Zinfandel, the mysterious red-wine grape of California.

Chardonnay The white-wine grape of Burgundy, Chardonnay contributes its characteristic buttery sensation to the wines of Chablis and Champagne also. As much a feeling as a taste, Chardonnay's full butteriness is balanced by an apple-like hardness and crisp acidity. The wine is commonly aged in small oak barrels, a practice that leaves a spicy trace of charred wood in the bouquet and flavor.

Riesling Also known as Johannisberg Riesling, this grape produces the flowery, usually somewhat fruity wines of the Rhine valley. In *Spatlese* and *Auslese*, Riesling grapes reach intense, honey sweetness due to the effects of *Botrytis cinerea*, the "noble rot," a skin fungus that sucks water from the grape and intensifies sugar and flavor. In Alsace, Rieslings are also vinted, though in a drier style than the typical Rhinewine of Germany.

Cabernet Sauvignon The red-wine grape of Bordeaux, Cabernet Sauvignon makes a full-bodied wine that requires long cellar-aging to soften brash tannin. In a balanced wine, the taste of raspberry or blackberry fruit often shines through, offset by herbal overtones. Oak aging can lend a cigar-box or cedar-chest quality to its bouquet. The grape's tendency toward forwardness nearly always begs for blending with a softer relative, such as Merlot.

Pinot Noir The red-wine grape of the northern part of Burgundy, Pinot Noir also plays a significant role in making champagne. With legions of fans who cheer this grape as the number one red-wine variety in the world, the best vintages are smooth and lightly perfumed. Scents of supple leather or cherries may rise from its bouquet. With less tannin than Cabernet Sauvignon, Pinot Noir often earns the adjective of elegant.

NATIVE GRAPE VARIETIES

As disease-resistant rootstock or as breeding stock, American species have played a major role in the world of wine. Only one species, *Vitis rotundifolia*, makes drinkable wine without *vinifera* influence, called scuppernong or muscadine, a wine associated with the southern Atlantic states. All other so-called ''native grapes'' evolved as varieties either through chance pollination with *vinifera* or by the intentional experiments of humans.

As wine grapes, the native varieties differ from *vinifera* beyond their general resistance to many endemic diseases and their foxy character. Largely due to the short growing season in which these American varieties survive as no others can, native grapes show low sugar content compared to the *vinifera* of California. For years California state laws have prohibited the addition of sweeteners. East of the Rockies, as well as in northern France and Germany, ''chaptalization'' is a common way to boost alcohol content by providing added nutrients for the yeast to consume. The process derives its name from Jean-Antoine Chaptal, Napoleon's minister of the interior, who, in 1801 brought winemaking into the Enlightened

Age with his *Traité sur La Vigne*.

The following lists treat separately varieties found in the wild from varieties bred with a purpose in mind. Many experts consider members of the latter group, such as Elvira, Missouri Riesling, Niagara, and Delaware, to be native varieties, offspring of American parents. The recorded history of these grapes, however, suggests that they are actually engineered "American hybrids," and, thus, suitable for inclusion in the "hybrid varieties" section that follows.

Catawba (V. labrusca) In the 1820s Revolutionary War hero Maj. John Adlum (1759-1836) of Maryland cultivated Catawba cuttings that he pruned from a neighbor's garden. Supposing that the vines had come from North Carolina, he named them after the Catawba River there. He sent one of his early Catawba vintages to his friend, former president Thomas Jefferson, in 1823. Jefferson, who strongly advocated the cultivation of native grapes as a matter of national pride, regarded Adlum's Catawba as "truly a fine wine, of high flavour."

Discouraged by his initial plantings of *vinifera* and Alexander grapes, Nicholas Longworth (1783-1863) of Cincinnati ordered Catawba cuttings from Adlum in 1825. In the next twenty-five years, the reputation of Longworth's Catawba spread worldwide, particularly as America's first champagne. An English writer in 1858 pronounced it to be "a finer wine of the hock species and flavour than any hock that comes from the Rhine." The American poet Henry Wadsworth Longfellow praised the Catawba in verse; and the Ohio River valley became known as "America's Rhineland."

Longworth's glory, based on the remarkable success of the Catawba, evaporated in the 1860s, as disease and pests ravaged his vineyards and the family members who survived him split up and sold the vineyards they had inherited.

Isabella (V. labrusca) William R. Prince (1795-1869), a horticulturist from New York, believed that the cuttings of this vine that his father received originated in South Carolina. Named for the wife of amateur wine-grower Col. George Gibbs, the Isabella became almost as widely planted as Catawba before the Civil War. In

Hermann, Jacob Fugger vinted this grape to contribute to the city's first vintage in 1848. Regarded as one of the more promising *Phylloxera*-resistant rootstocks, cuttings of Isabella traveled worldwide, leading some viticulturists to estimate that it is currently the most widely grown grape variety. The importance of Prince to American viticulture was also secured by his 1830 work, *Treatise on the Vine*, the first such book written by an American-born author.

***Concord* (V. labrusca)** In 1849 Ephraim Wales Bull (1805-1895) of Concord, Massachusetts, propagated an amazingly prolific and hardy vine from wild *labrusca* seeds he had gathered near his home. Three years later he exhibited the Concord to the Massachusetts Horticultural Society. Cuttings spread quickly across the southern shore of Lake Erie, arriving in Missouri before 1860. More than the Alexander, Isabella, and Catawba, the Concord heralded the dawn of commercial winemaking in America. For Bull, the vine's greatest strength, its ease of cultivation and propagation, was its most heartbreaking fault. Horticulturists spread cuttings of Concord just as modern-day software pirates share bootlegged computer programs. Bull realized virtually no income from his discovery.

Hermann's George Husmann received "a few eyes" of Concord from Jasper G. Soulard of Galena, Illinois, in 1855. In the second edition of his *American Grape Growing and Wine Making* (1885) Husmann wrote of the Concord:

> Will, with skillful handling and a little artificial heat, make a wine of fair quality, of very enlivening and invigorating character, which is emphatically the "poor man's" drink, as it can be produced cheap, and is just the beverage he needs, instead of the poisonous compounds called whiskey and brandy.

***Norton* (V. aestavalis)** Once regarded as the best grape in the world for making red wine, Norton's Virginia Seedling was cultivated by Dr. Daniel Norton of Richmond, Virginia. Norton believed this vine to be a chance cross between the *vinifera* Miller's Burgundy and the Bland grape, a *labrusca* variety. However, critics of this genealogy pointed out that these parents did not flower at the same time, making cross pollination unlikely. The controversy of the plant's origins, like that of California's Zinfandel, cloaked this grape in mystery. The fact that its wine showed no trace of foxiness also helped to make it a grape of promise.

George Husmann recalled that Norton's Virginia Seedling arrived in Hermann around 1848. While Friedrich Muench's rendition varies in some details from the Husmann account, the stories of Norton's Virginia Seedling reflect the wide-spread enthusiasm about the grape and demonstrate the interest Missouri grape growers had in new varieties.

The Hermann winegrowers who cultivated Norton's Virginia Seedling, led by Jacob Rommel, sought an evaluation of one of their early vintages from Nicholas Longworth, recognized in his time as "the father of American grape culture." Repeating his earlier dim assessment of the Norton grape, Longworth judged the wine to be unpleasant. Husmann took the opposite stance on the Norton's future:

> There is, perhaps, no other grape which has given such uniform satisfaction as this, and although I have warmly praised and recommended it from the first, I have seen no reason to retract a single word which I have said in its favor.

> Makes, perhaps, the best medicinal wine in the country; it has already saved thousands of lives, especially of children suffering with summer complaint, and acquired a world-wide reputation. Even as a table grape, many prefer it on account of its spicy character, and its plump bunches will keep like winter apples.

***Cynthiana* (V. aestivalis)** Like that of the Norton, the source of the Cynthiana lurks in mystery, due in part to its resemblance to the former. Most horticulturists, including Husmann, traced the origins of this grape to the Red River area of Arkansas. He said he received cuttings of Cynthiana from William R. Prince in 1858. From its introduction, debate centered on the differences between the Cynthiana and its "twin," Norton. Comparing the two varieties of *aestivalis*, Husmann described the Cynthiana thus:

> [Its] bunch is generally heavier, with broader shoulders, the berry somewhat larger, sweeter, and less astringent, and the wine is not quite as dark, less rough and astringent, without that coffee-like taste of the Norton, and much more spicy and delicate, resembling the best Burgundy.

Many Missouri winemakers believed that Cynthiana would become America's grape for good red wine. In 1883, the *Bushberg Catalogue* proudly announced that the Isidor Bush & Son & Meissner Cynthiana had won the First Medal of Merit at the world exposition in Vienna. The next year French experts at the Congres de Montpellier voiced unequivocal praise. They described the Cynthiana of Mr. Bush as "a red wine of fine color, rich in body and alcohol, reminding us of old Roussillon wine," an accolade they also bestowed on the wine of "Poschel & Sherer," the founders of Hermann's Stone Hill Wine Company.

HYBRID VARIETIES

Toward the end of the nineteenth century horticulturists in America and Europe explored ways to improve grape varieties through hybridization. Several conditions of the time spurred their efforts. In America, viticulturists realized the tremendous potential of this country for producing unlimited amounts of wine. To tap this potential, grape breeders sought to develop plants that could withstand deep-freeze winters and endemic diseases, and yield wine without the trademark foxy flavor of *labrusca* grapes.

At his home base in Denison, Texas, T. V. Munson (1843-1913) developed over three hundred hybrids, two of which he named for his colleagues Friedrich Munch and Hermann Jaeger. In Missouri, Jaeger directed his attention to *Phylloxera*-resistant varieties that he developed in his vineyard in Neosho. The early prospects of hybridizing techniques were realized by Friedrich Muench as he developed varieties that he named White Home, Little Ozark, Ozark Seedling, and Big Ozark. At Hermann, George Husmann also carried out cross pollination and grafting experiments to come up with a grape that favored winemaking requirements. The vines of one his experiments, named Dry Hill Beauty, survive in his vineyard east of Hermann to this day.

For the most part, these American hybrids became merely obscure references in the vineyardists' notebooks. The onset of Prohibition stilled further research in America and nearly erased the life's work of these scientists. A few varieties escaped the purge to produce wine in Missouri after Prohibition, such as Munson's Muench grape, Jacob Rommel's Elvira, and Nicholas Grein's Missouri Riesling.

In those early days of plant hybridization, the process of developing a new plant strain took years, perhaps decades or generations. The standard vineyard procedure prescribed the surgical cross-pollination of two grape plants. The seeds that resulted from this marriage carried some characteristics of both plants. The results could not be determined until viable plant hybrids survived; and then, only after several years of cultivation would the plant inform the winemaker if its fruit had any chance of making acceptable wine. Seeds of the experimental plants were planted; seedlings that showed promise, perhaps one in ten, were continued, the others destroyed. From the selected survivors, cuttings were taken and rooted, yielding plants identical to the seedlings.

In Europe the devastation caused by *Phylloxera* provided an urgent impetus to develop varieties that could survive the pest's attack. As Missouri state entomologist Charles V. Riley (1843-95) had proposed, American rootstock could shield the European varieties from subsoil infestation. However, grafting was an expensive and labor-intensive process. A group of French horticulturists believed that hybridization might create new answers to the problem. Viable hybrids, called *producteurs directs* because they grew on their own roots, had to go through several generations of cultivation to achieve results. Yet, as necessity inspired invention, the *Phylloxera* crisis in France sired a new generation of botanists and ushered in an era of unprecedented genetic engineering. Even though they had received but scant attention in the United States prior to Prohibition, the hybrids were poised to restock America's barren vineyards, particularly east of the Rockies, at the first breath of Repeal.

Philip Wagner, a Maryland newspaperman, and his wife, Jocelyn, had dabbled in home winemaking at the close of the "noble experiment." In 1933, the year that Prohibition ended, he published *American Wines and How to Make Them*, a book that inspired many winemaking enthusiasts to entertain new hopes for the future of winemaking in the eastern United States. An assignment in Europe during World War II exposed Wagner to the tremendous advance in viticulture that had taken place in France during America's period of dormancy. In the mid-1940s, the Wagners collected hybrid cuttings from the gardens of various amateur winemakers in the eastern states and soon had a thriving hybrid vineyard of their own, which they named Boordy Vineyard. Although the first edition of Wagner's *American Wines* did not mention hybrids, later versions incorporated the theme as a call to the conviction that hybrids could make fine wine.

At the opposite end of the spectrum from Konstantin Frank, the staunch critic of hybrids, Philip and Jocelyn Wagner had faith in the ability of hybrids to withstand existing climate and soil conditions in the eastern states and to produce fine wine. A blind tasting validated their convictions. Among winemaker friends who gathered from time to time to sample each other's wares, Wagner secretly introduced into the competition a bottle of wine he had vinted from hybrid grapes. His friends hardly believed that the wine—which they called crisp and complex, lacking in foxiness—had come from French hybrids. Soon after proving his point, Wagner retired from the newspaper business to devote himself full-time to growing hybrids and making wine.

Following the lead of the French, state agricultural colleges and reseach facilities now fund extensive grape research. At facilities such as the New York State Agricultural Experiment Station in Geneva and Missouri's State Fruit Experiment Station in Mountain Grove, agronomists seek new hybrids that can take advantage of growing conditions in the eastern United States. Two premises guide their work: that they have yet to find the grape that will become for their own locales what the Chardonnay and Pinot Noir are to Burgundy; and that viticulture can be a profitable form of agriculture in the United States.

The list that follows begins with nineteenth-century American hybrids that many viticulturists classify as native grapes. The French hybrids, often call French-American hybrids in recognition of a genealogy traced back to Hermann Jaeger and his colleagues, were developed in France. Other hybrids, such as Cayuga and Steuben, have been developed in this country.

American hybrids

Elvira Most histories of winemaking in America credit Jacob Rommel of Hermann with developing this cross between *Vitis riparia* and *labrusca* parents. According to the local history of Gasconade County, however, Jacob Rommel, Jr., born in Philadelphia in 1837 and the son of the man who walked from St. Louis to Hermann in January 1839, produced this grape in his father's nursery around 1880. In his 1885 work, *American Grape Growing and Wine Making*, George Husmann states that Jacob Rommel's Elvira first bore fruit in 1869.

In any case, Husmann lauded the vine for its hardiness to withstand the worst of Missouri winter temperatures, its resistance to disease, its high productivity, and its ability to yield fine wine. This last attribute Husmann described as "a beautiful greenish-yellow wine, without foxiness, and a delicate and full aroma, resembling Riesling."

Missouri Riesling Another pioneering viticulturist in Hermann, Nicholas "Papa" Grein, also crossed a *riparia* seedling, this one known as Taylor, with a *labrusca* variety. The resulting hybrid, Missouri Riesling, resembled its German namesake only in the color of its wine. About Missouri Riesling, Husmann wrote that it was "said to make an exquisite white wine."

Delaware Named for Delaware, Ohio, this grape originated from the work of American horticulturists E. S. Rogers and Jacob Moore. Husmann, however, wrote in 1866 that A. Thompson developed the grape in his Delaware, Ohio, vineyards, a genealogy with some basis in fact since Rogers and Moore conducted their work in Massachusetts and New York. Other plant historians have taken the position that the Delaware, a chance cross between *labrusca* and *vinifera* parents, was the last native variety found in the wild.

Nonetheless, from its nineteenth-century origins to the present, eager winemakers have used the Delaware in their wines. Husmann described it as "a nice little grape, sweet and luscious for the table, and makes a fine wine." Friedrich Muench, meanwhile, said Delaware "makes our best and most fiery white wine, which is very like the finest Rhinewine."

Niagara The Niagara was developed in 1868 and embraced by the Niagara Juice Company. Husmann described it as a cross between Concord and Cassady, another American hybrid. In his notes he pictured its berry as "large, slightly oblong, semi-transparent, greenish-white, bronzed in sun, adheres well to the bunch, flesh tender, sweet and melting, good flavor, skin tough, and bears handling well."

Muench One of T. V. Munson's creations, the Muench grape produces a crisp, dry red wine. Its family history likely stems from the marriage of South Carolina's Herbemont and the post oak grape of the Mississippi Valley. Herbemont derives its name from Nicholas Herbemont, the man credited with discovering this sun-loving member of *Vitis aestivalis* in the woods around Columbia, South Carolina. The American species *Vitis lincecumii*, known as the post oak grape, also favored the southern climate where Herbemont lived. This species was used extensively as breeding stock by Munson and by Missouri's Hermann Jaeger.

French-American hybrids

Seyval From the grape developed by Seyve-Villard (1895-1959), Seyval blanc wine is often called the "Chardonnay of the East," perhaps more for its marketing potential to vineyards east of the Rockies than for its similarity to the classic grape of Burgundy or the claim to fame of California. Typically, it more closely resembles Sauvignon Blanc of the Loire Valley. Its creator was the son of another famous French hybridizer; in 1919, Seyve married the daughter of Victor Villard, joining his bride's maiden name with his own, a not-uncommon practice in France.

Vidal Dry Vidal wine will perhaps remind one more of a white Burgundy—that is, Chardonnay—than a Seyval. J. L. Vidal, who directed the Fougerat Station at Bois-Charentes and studied at the Ecole Nationale Agronomique in Montpellier, France, created this grape from the Ugni Blanc *vinifera*. Wine made from Vidal grapes often has the luscious, buttery fullness of a Chardonnay more than the crispness of a Seyval. Many inexperienced tasters overlook this varietal because its nose does not demand immediate attention. While its first impression often only tickles the olfactory fancy, a lingering finish embeds a well-made Vidal in the memory taste buds. Its use in blends makes Vidal perhaps the most widely planted wine grape in France.

Vignoles Previously known as Ravat 51 after its creator J. F. Ravat (d. 1940), the Vignoles shows a particular fondness for Missouri's soil and climate. Part of its ancestry includes Chardonnay and a hybrid developed by Hermann Jaeger. In ever-increasing numbers, winemakers are being won over to the winter-hardy Vignoles. Its versatility lends this grape to produce dry as well as off-dry wines more than any other hybrid in the state. In dry wines, the nose and taste are dramatic and the finish is complex. In off-dry versions, Vignoles appeals to the senses with scents of apricots or peaches, prompting Frank England, winemaker of O'Vallon Winery, to call it "Missouri's noble grape."

Rayon d'Or As Seibel 4986, this white-wine grape was one of Albert Seibel's (1844-1936) early hybrids. Through an intermediary, Seibel received seeds of Hermann Jaeger's American hybrids in 1886. With these seeds Seibel resumed his grape hybrid research in the St. Julien vineyards of Bordeaux, numbering his new creations from the beginning.

Not as famous as some of Seibel's red-wine hybrids, Rayon d'Or has received limited attention by Missouri's winemakers. Nonetheless, Philip Wagner regarded it as a prolific vine producing grapes with a well-balanced sugar and acid content.

Villard Noir* and *Villard Blanc This red-wine grape creation of Seyve-Villard, originally known as Seyve-Villard 18315, was described by Philip Wagner in his *Grapes Into Wine* of 1976 as capable of making a "firm, well-balanced wine." Mostly used in proprietary blends, as a varietal the wine can approach a favorable comparison with Merlot in terms of body. Seyve-Villard's white hybrid counterpart, noted as Seyve-Villard 12375, excells in producing fruit, yet is susceptible to crown gall and winter injury.

Chelois A creation of Albert Seibel, Chelois once piqued the hopes of Missouri winemakers to produce a notable red wine. Known in Seibel's lab book as Seibel 10878, Chelois has won comparison to the red wine of Burgundy. From Kansas City to St. Louis, wine lovers enjoy debating how to pronounce this exotic name. In general, Missourians around St. Louis prefer the pronuciation that rhymes with Illinois. Elsewhere, wine lovers turn the word into an interrogative of disbelief, "she'll wha'?"

Like other red-wine hybrid grapes, however, Seibel 10878 usually makes a high-acid wine when bottled as a varietal. In addition, initial excitement about the grape diminished as its susceptibility to crown gall became known. As a result, acreage in Missouri declined after 1985.

Chancellor Another of Seibel's creations from his St. Julien vineyard in France's Bordeaux region, Chancellor (Seibel 7053) for a time was enthusiastically vinted by Missouri winemakers. Its tendency toward prominent acid content and the public's unwillingness to cellar red wine for adequate time combined to earn only casual interest of consumers. Nonetheless, Chancellor remains a widely planted grape in Missouri, finding its way into many proprietary blends. Vinted in a *nouveau* style, the grape yields an appealing red table wine that does not require years of age to soften its inherent acids. The wine accompanies tomato-based sauces, broiled salmon, and smoked turkey very well.

Chambourcin Developed by Joannes Seyve (1900-1966),

the brother of Seyve-Villard, this red-wine grape (Joannes Seyve 26-205) can also be vinted in a light and fruity *nouveau* style. Typically it produces a deeply colored wine with hues of blue. Though it has been susceptible to severe crown gall infestation, its promise as Missouri's red-wine grape encouraged winegrowers to accept it as a leading candidate for their vineyards.

Baco Noir Known as Baco #1, this hybrid was one of the first grapes planted on a commercial scale in vineyards east of the Rockies after Repeal. Reflecting the tastes and background of its creator, Maurice Baco, wine of this grape can compare favorably with Cabernet Sauvignon, the principal red-wine grape of Bordeaux. In Missouri plantings of Baco Noir declined as winemakers turned their attention to Chambourcin and Chancellor, the wines of which typically require less aging than Baco Noir to soften tannic acid.

American French-American hybrids

Cayuga The State Agricultural Experiment Station in Geneva, New York, developed the Cayuga grape (Geneva White #3) in 1945, naming it after one of the nearby Finger Lakes. Generally vinted off-dry, Cayuga's genealogy includes Seyval Blanc and Schuyler, the latter a cross between Zinfandel and Ontario grapes.

Steuben Also developed at the Geneva station, the Steuben's lavender grape is most frequently used to blend white wine.

Bob Scheef was born in Bonne Terre, Missouri, and raised in Webster Groves. He spent fifteen years looking for someplace better than home. Following five years in San Francisco, where he learned to appreciate wine, he happily returned to St. Louis in 1989. Happily, too, he discovered that a full-blown wine industry had blossomed in his home state. With keen interest he now studies Missouri, the fascinating subject he spurned as a public school pupil. This is his first book.